Table of Contents

CHAPTER 1

Cooking with Coconut

COCONUT LOVER'S COOKBOOK

4th Edition

Bruce Fife, N.D.

Piccadilly Books, Ltd.
Colorado Springs, CO

Piccadilly Books, Ltd.
P.O. Box 25203
Colorado Springs, CO 80936
info@piccadillybooks.com
www.piccadillybooks.com

Library of Congress Cataloging-in-Publication Data

Fife, Bruce, 1952-
   Coconut lovers cookbook / Bruce Fife.
        p.cm.
      ISBN-13 978-0-941599-87-0
      1. Cookery (Coconut) I. Title.
   TX814.2.C63F54 2004
   641.6'.461--dc22   2004040026

Printed in the USA

INTRODUCTION

This book was written for people who love coconut. It was also written for the growing number of health conscious individuals who recognize coconut as a marvelous health food and want to gain the many health benefits it provides.

Of particular interest is coconut oil, which has gained a reputation in recent years as a super health food. It is considered by nutritionists to be among the healthiest of all dietary oils. People who want to take advantage of the health benefits of coconut oil will find this book a blessing. It contains many creative ways to add the oil into the diet using a variety of delicious recipes.

Every recipe in this book contains coconut in one form or another, whether it's coconut meat, milk, or oil. A large number of the recipes in this book, such as the Cheese Cups and Sesame Chicken Salad, are completely original and found in no other source. Some of the recipes are variations on popular non-coconut dishes, such as Chicken A La King, using coconut milk in place of dairy. And, of course, this book wouldn't be complete without old favorites, such as Coconut Cream Pie and Coconut Macaroons.

Many people who live in non-coconut growing regions of the world mistakenly think of coconut as just an ingredient for making desserts and sweets. Coconut, however, is very versatile and can be used in a variety of ways other than desserts. In this book there are recipes for creating savory main dishes, appetizing side dishes, satisfying snacks, and nutritious beverages. You will find a number of coconut oil- and coconut milk-based salad dressings that go well with both fruit and vegetable salads. You will also find recipes for creamy soups and hearty chowders, delicious curries, stews, and casseroles. You could literally eat coconut with every meal without consuming a single dessert. Of course, if you like desserts, you will find plenty here to choose from, including cakes, pies, puddings, and ice cream.

Concerned about sugar? No problem. All the dessert recipes can be made using natural sweeteners of your choice. In addition to the regular recipes, also included are reduced sugar versions. Many of these recipes can be made with very little sugar or none at all. Some of the reduced sugar recipes use stevia extract—a non-caloric herbal sweetener. Stevia makes an excellent non-caloric replacement for sugar or artificial sweeteners when used in combination with fruit and other naturally sweet foods.

Many people ask: is coconut high in carbohydrate? If you're on a low-carbohydrate diet, you're in luck. Coconut contains very little effective (i.e., digestible) carbohydrate. Although coconut meat is mildly sweet, it is composed primarily of indigestible fiber and, therefore, is a low-carbohydrate, high-fiber food. Coconut milk, likewise, has very little carbohydrate, and coconut oil has none.

As a nutritionist, I prefer to use the healthiest ingredients possible, choosing whole wheat flour over white, brown rice over white, and natural sweeteners over highly processed or artificial sugars. However, I've made allowances in the recipes for those readers who don't want to go all natural.

MY FAVORITE RECIPES

I like all of the recipes in this book. If I didn't, they wouldn't be here. While writing this book, I experimented with hundreds of recipes, adding and combining different ingredients to create a variety of appetizing coconut based meals and beverages. Many of these recipes are completely of my own creation. Those that were based on existing recipes were usually modified to include coconut in one form or another. In compiling this book, I tried to include a variety of foods to suit a variety of tastes. A few, however, are my favorites. While we all have different tastes, I think most people would enjoy these just as much as I do. For this reason, I have included this symbol ♥ next to those recipes that are my favorites. I think you'll like them too.

Before making any of the recipes in this book, you should read the section titled *Read Me First* that follows. It contains important information that will help you understand and use the recipes in this book to your best advantage. It will also clarify meanings of terms used in the recipes.

READ ME FIRST

Before making any of the recipes in this book, read this section first. The information below explains terms commonly used in the recipes that follow. *It is important that you read this material to avoid possible confusion.*

Dried Coconut

Dried coconut is sold under a number of descriptive terms such as desiccated, shredded, grated, flaked, angle flaked, etc. These terms can be confusing, especially since they are often used interchangeably. Therefore, it is important

6

that you know what types of coconut to use in the recipes. In order to avoid confusion and make recipes consistent, I use three terms to describe three different types of dried coconut. Because there is no standard terminology, these terms are not necessarily the same as those used by food producers or other cookbook authors. In this book, I refer to three types of dried coconut: flaked, shredded, and grated. When I say *flaked* coconut, I mean coconut that is in flakes. *Shredded* coconut is like what you would get if you used a grater to shred it. *Grated* coconut is very finely shredded or grated coconut. In essence, the difference between them is primarily size—flaked coconut being the largest and grated the smallest.

Most of the dried coconut in grocery stores is sweetened and contain preservatives. The recipes in this book use *unsweetened* coconut. If your local grocery store does not carry unsweetened coconut without preservatives, you can get it in health food stores or see the Resource Directory at the end of this book.

Most of the recipes in this book call for grated coconut. If you don't have grated coconut available, generally shredded or flaked coconut will do.

Cooking With Coconut Oil

One of the purposes of using oil in cooking is to prevent food from sticking to cookware. Coconut oil is one of the healthiest cooking oils because it is very stable under normal cooking temperatures and does not oxidize or degrade like other vegetable oils. However, for pan frying or baking, it is not as effective as most other oils in preventing foods from sticking. To improve the non-sticking property of coconut oil for frying or baking, you can mix another oil, such as olive oil, with coconut oil.

The healthiest and most effective non-stick cooking oil I have found is a mixture of coconut oil and liquid lecithin. This is absolutely the best cooking oil you can use. It's the only oil I use to prevent foods from sticking. Use the oil to coat baking dishes and bread pans. A thin layer is all that is needed to do the job. This combination is so effective, bread almost pops out of the pan. Clean up is a breeze as well: no sticking or burning, so pans easily wipe clean. No scrubbing or harsh cleansing pads needed. Once you begin to use this oil, you won't want to use any other in your baking ever again. You can find liquid lecithin at your local health food store and on the Internet. To make the non-stick oil simply mix ¼ cup of melted coconut oil with ½ teaspoon of liquid lecithin. This recipe makes enough non-stick cooking oil for many baking projects. Use what you need and store the remainder in the refrigerator for future use. It will last for many months.

Sugar and Sweeteners

You can use a variety of sweeteners for the recipes in this book, many of which are interchangeable. When the term "sugar" is used in a recipe, you can use white granulated sugar or any other *dry* sugar such as sucanat (dried sugarcane juice), date sugar, palm sugar, or dehydrated maple syrup. If the term "honey" is used in a recipe, you can substitute maple syrup, corn syrup, rice syrup, or any other *liquid* sweetener. A few recipes offer variations in which powdered stevia extract is used in place of either a dry or wet sweetener. This extract is a natural, non-caloric sweetener derived from the stevia herb.

Most of the recipes for sweets in this book include both full sugar and reduced sugar versions. So you can choose the one you prefer. Some of the reduced sugar recipes use no added sugar, relying only on fruit, coconut, and/or stevia. Stevia is essentially calorie free. It is about 200 times sweeter than table sugar, so only a little bit is needed to achieve the same level of sweetness. The major drawback with stevia is that if you use too much, it produces a bitter aftertaste. So for most recipes, you cannot replace *all* of the sugar with stevia. For best results, combine stevia with other sweeteners. This way, you can significantly reduce the total amount of sugar called for in many recipes. For example, you can reduce the sugar content in a recipe by half if you replace the other half with a little stevia. You will still achieve a sweet taste with only half the sugar.

If the recipe includes fruit, you can often eliminate all the sugar and use stevia instead. The fruit provides just enough natural sweetening to complement the stevia so that together they provide all the sweetness necessary.

One half teaspoon of stevia has the sweetening effect of 1 cup of granulated sugar. If a recipe asks for 1 cup of sugar you can reduce the sugar to ½ cup and add ¼ teaspoon of powdered stevia extract to achieve the same level of sweetness. When you substitute stevia for a small amount of sugar, be careful to use just a tiny bit. A little can go a long way and too much can give the food an overpowering aftertaste. If you are not accustomed to using stevia, it may take a little practice to find just the right amount to use to suit your taste. Stevia extract is available at most health food stores. No artificial sweeteners are used in any of the recipes in this book.

Whole Grains

As a nutritionist, I strongly recommend the use of whole grains over processed, refined grains and flours. For this reason, the recipes in this book use whole grains whenever possible. When the word "flour" is used, I mean "whole wheat" flour; however, if you prefer, you can use white flour in most of these recipes. When the word "rice" is used, I mean brown rice. In most cases you may use either brown or white rice. When it is important to use one or the other, a distinction will be made.

> No artificial sweeteners or hydrogenated vegetable oils are used in any of the recipes in this book.

COCONUT PRODUCTS

Coconut, as the name implies, is a nut, or actually, a seed. Unlike most other nuts, the coconut is the source of several food products. Besides the meat, you have coconut water, coconut milk, coconut cream, and coconut oil. In coconut growing regions of the world these products are used to make a variety of foods such as coconut wine, vinegar, butter, sugar, and more. Most of these more exotic coconut products are not readily available outside their native lands. The recipes in this book use coconut products that are readily available at your local supermarket or health food store. These products include coconut meat (fresh and dried), coconut milk and cream, and coconut oil. Coconut water is becoming increasingly popular and a few recipes have been included.

COCONUT MEAT
How to Choose A Good Coconut

Fresh coconuts are available at most grocery stores and Asian markets. The quality of fresh coconuts varies greatly even in the same store. The age of the coconuts and how they are handled greatly affects quality. Coconuts that have been battered around and cracked spoil very quickly. Once a crack occurs in the shell, mold quickly develops inside. Most coconuts are shipped long distances over extended periods of time. You have no way of telling how old

9

they are when you buy them. The older they are, the more likely they are to be moldy.

You can identify mold when you break open the coconut and see yellow or brown coloring in the meat, or smell an off odor. Sometimes you can smell mold on the outside of the coconut before breaking it open.

When choosing a fresh coconut, look for one without any cracks. If the coconut is damp or has wet spots, it means the shell is cracked and the coconut water is leaking. Shake the coconut to detect the swishing sound of the coconut water. If there is little or no water in the coconut, it is old. Avoid those with white spots, particularly around the "eyes." The white is mold that has probably developed from water leaking from a tiny crack.

Even after you follow these guidelines there is no guarantee that you won't get a moldy coconut. But at least your chances of getting a decent one are greatly increased. After you buy a coconut and bring it home, don't leave it on the countertop; store it in the refrigerator. The older it gets, the more likely it will go bad. So keep it refrigerated and eat it as soon as possible.

How to Open A Coconut

To open a coconut, first puncture *two* of the "eyes" and drain the water. Coconuts have three eyes. One of the eyes is soft and very easy to puncture, the other two are a bit more difficult. I use an ice pick. You may also use a hammer and nail. After draining the liquid, hold the coconut securely on a hard surface and hit it with a hammer. Coconut shells are very hard so you will need to put some force into it.

Another way to crack a coconut shell is to place the coconut on a baking sheet and heat it in the oven for 20 minutes at 400 degrees F. After it is heated, tap the coconut all over to loosen meat, then crack it with a hammer.

Break the shell up into several pieces. With a table knife, you can pry the meat off the shell. The meat will have a brown membrane or skin on it where it was in contact with the shell. You can trim this off with a vegetable peeler. If you see any brown or yellow discoloration in the white meat, it is mold. Small patches of mold can be cut off and discarded. Most coconuts will have a spot or two. If a lot of discoloration is present, throw the whole thing away.

Fresh coconut makes a wonderful snack. Many of the recipes in this book call for grated or shredded coconut. You can make grated or shredded coconut with a grater. One medium-size coconut will give you 3 to 4 cups of shredded coconut. When measuring shredded coconut for recipes, do not pack the measure.

Generally, dried coconut is used in most recipes. This is the way packaged coconut is usually sold. Coconut is dried to extend shelf life. Drying does not alter its nutritional value. Only water is removed. Dried coconut will remain edible for a couple of months. It is a good idea, however, to keep it refrigerated or frozen.

You can dry freshly grated coconut in a dehydrator or put it in on a cookie sheet in the oven for a couple of hours at low heat. Store unused coconut in an airtight container in the refrigerator. Fresh coconut spoils quickly, so eat it within about five days. If you store it in the freezer, it will last about six months.

Dietary Fiber

Although fresh coconut is slightly sweet, it is a low carbohydrate food. Coconut meat is composed mostly of non-digestible fiber with a fair amount of water and oil. It contains very little digestible carbohydrate. The fiber acts like a broom, sweeping the intestinal contents along the digestive tract, aiding in elimination and helping to reduce digestive problems such a constipation, colitis, and even colon cancer. Coconut meat is one of the highest natural sources of dietary fiber. I don't know of any food with a higher fiber content. It has more fiber than either oat bran or wheat bran and tastes a whole lot better! If you need to add fiber to your diet, coconut meat is an excellent way to do it.

Foods contain two types of carbohydrate: digestible and non-digestible. Digestible carbohydrate consists of starch and sugar and provides calories. Non-digestible carbohydrate is the fiber and provides no calories.

According to the U.S. Department of Agriculture, 24 percent of the carbohydrate in oat bran is composed of fiber. Wheat bran is 42 percent fiber. Soybeans contain only 29 percent fiber. Coconut beats them all. Its carbohydrate content is composed of a whopping 75 percent fiber!

Nutritionists recommend that we get between 20 to 35 grams of fiber a day. This is 2 to 3 times higher than the average intake, which is about 14 grams a day. One cup of dried shredded coconut (unpacked) contains 12 grams of fiber. One 2 x 2-inch piece of fresh coconut contains 5 grams of fiber. Adding fresh or dried coconut to your diet can significantly improve your daily fiber intake.

Coconut Flour

Coconut flour is made from finely ground, defatted, and dehydrated coconut meat. It has a much higher fiber content than any other flour. It contains no gluten—the protein found in wheat and many other grains. Because of this it is ideal for people who are sensitive to gluten or allergic to wheat. Although coconut flour doesn't have gluten, it does not lack protein. It has as much protein as whole wheat flour. Coconut flour can be used to make a variety of baked goods including bread, muffins, cakes, pies, and cookies.

Coconut flour looks and feels much like wheat flour, but it doesn't cook the same. For this reason, you cannot use coconut flour in recipes designed for wheat flour. It just won't work. I do not include any coconut flour recipes in this book. However, if you are interested in coconut flour recipes I have an entire book devoted to this topic. It's titled *Cooking With Coconut Flour: A Delicious Low-Carb, Gluten-Free Alternative to Wheat*. If you are allergic to wheat, gluten intolerant, on a low-carb diet, or just want to increase your fiber intake, you should take a look at this book.

COCONUT WATER

Contrary to popular belief, the liquid inside a fresh coconut is *not* coconut milk. This liquid is known as *coconut water* or *coconut juice*. Coconut water is a relatively clear, sweet tasting liquid. Coconut milk, on the other hand, is manufactured by squeezing or extracting the liquid from coconut meat.

Coconut water is very different from coconut milk in taste and content. Because of its sweetness, it is usually consumed as a beverage. It has a delicious flavor all its own and not really like coconut meat. In addition to natural sugars, it also contains a complex array of minerals and electrolytes, which have made it popular as a sports drink.

The electrolyte profile of coconut water is similar to human plasma and for that reason it has been used by doctors as an intravenous solution and injected directly into the bloodstream to prevent dehydration. Doctors working in tropical climates have often used the water from coconuts as IV solutions. This practice was common during World War II and in Vietnam where commercial

IV solutions were often in short supply. Coconut water has become popular as a natural sports rehydration beverage.

The taste of coconut water varies depending on the age of the coconut. The water from fresh green (immature) coconuts is regarded as the best in taste and quality. The water from mature coconuts, although good, doesn't compare. Until recently, just about the only way to get coconut water was to crack open a fresh coconut. Coconut water is now available commercially in bottled and tetra pak containers.

Because of its sweetness, coconut water can be used to sweeten other beverages such as fruit smoothies and blender drinks. Unlike most other coconut products, the water contains virtually no fat.

COCONUT MILK

Coconut milk is made from squeezing the juice out of coconut meat. It is distinctly different from coconut water and has far more uses. This coconut meat extract has a milky white color, creamy texture, and nutty flavor. Coconut milk contains about 17 to 24 percent fat, which gives it its characteristic creamy taste and texture. Unlike coconut water, it is not sweet and, for this reason, can be used to make a variety of delicious soups, stews, sauces, curries, gravies, and desserts. Coconut milk can be used in place of dairy milk or cream in many recipes.

Canned coconut milk is available in many grocery and health food stores. It is most commonly sold in 14-ounce cans but is also available in larger cans as well as cartons. In addition to coconut milk, you can also find coconut cream, which has a slightly higher fat content. Don't confuse coconut milk or coconut cream with *cream of coconut*. Cream of coconut is coconut cream *with sugar added* and is very sweet. It is often used in beverages and desserts. Most of the recipes in this book use *unsweetened* coconut milk. If in doubt whether a brand of milk or cream has been sweetened, look at the ingredients label.

Some coconut milks have been watered down to reduce the fat content. This is called "low-fat" or "light" coconut milk. To retain the milk's thick texture, thickeners such as guar gum are added. I usually avoid low-fat milks because the coconut oil content is reduced. One of the reasons I eat a lot of coconut is to get the benefit of the fat. I don't want to reduce the benefit by eating low-fat coconut milk. In my opinion, the higher the fat content, the better.

When canned coconut milk sits on a shelf for any length of time, the cream often separates and floats to the top, particularly with brands that do not add thickeners. To mix the cream, simply shake the can vigorously before opening. Sometimes you may want to separate the cream from the watery liquid. You would do this if you need to use coconut cream in a recipe and only have coconut milk. In this case, don't shake the can. Open it and scrape the thick cream off the top. You can get more of the cream to separate by chilling the can in the refrigerator for a few days. The thickness of the cream varies from brand to brand, depending on fat content and the presence of thickening agents.

Coconut milk spoils quickly after it has been opened. When stored in an airtight container in the refrigerator, it will last for about four days. If frozen, it will last for six months or longer.

COCONUT OIL

You can use coconut oil in just about any recipe that calls for vegetable oil, shortening, butter, or margarine. Coconut oil is excellent for cooking. Unlike other vegetable oils, it is very stable when heated and does not create toxic byproducts. You can feel safe when you eat it, knowing that you aren't damaging your health. Coconut oil, however, has a moderate smoking point when used for frying, so you need to keep the temperature under 350 degrees F. If you don't have a temperature gauge on your stove, you can tell when it goes over this point because the oil will begin to smoke. This is a moderate temperature, but you can cook anything at this heat, even stir-fry vegetables. When coconut oil is used to grease pans or in baked goods, it can be cooked in the oven at higher temperature because evaporation of water in the food keeps the temperature lower.

Because coconut oil is very stable, it does not need to be refrigerated. It will stay fresh for at least two or three years unrefrigerated. If kept in a cool place, it will last even longer. This makes it an excellent storage oil. I buy it by the gallon so that I always have an ample supply.

Coconut oil melts at about 76 degrees F, becoming a clear liquid that looks like most any other vegetable oil. Below this temperature, it solidifies and takes on a creamy white appearance. At moderate room temperatures it has a soft buttery texture and is sometimes called coconut butter. If your kitchen is cooler than 76 degrees F, the oil will solidify. There is nothing wrong with this. Some people like to store the oil in the refrigerator. To liquefy the oil, simply immerse the bottom of the jar in hot water for a couple of minutes. The oil melts quickly.

Numerous processes are used to produce coconut oil, and the quality and taste of the oil varies from brand to brand. Two of the most popular types of coconut oil are virgin and expeller pressed. Virgin coconut oil has had minimal processing and retains a mild coconut taste and aroma. Expeller pressed coconut oil has undergone more processing and is essentially flavorless and odorless. Either oil can be used for any type of cooking or food preparation. Virgin coconut oil is preferred if you want to give foods a hint of coconut flavor. It generally is so mild that even moderately flavored foods will completely mask the coconut taste. For people who prefer not to have the coconut flavor in their food, expeller pressed oil is generally preferred.

A SUPERIOR HEALTH FOOD

Coconut meat is an excellent source of dietary fiber and is low in digestible carbohydrate. For this reason, coconut is great for low-carb diets or for those who need to restrict carbohydrate intake. Together coconut meat and water contain a nearly balanced supply of nutrients, which are capable of sustaining a person with little additional food for extended periods of time. Coconut water, the juice in fresh coconut, has long been known for its healing powers and is recommended for those with digestive problems. For decades doctors in Asia have used fresh coconut water as IV solutions. Athletes are now consuming it because it helps replenish electrolytes lost in perspiration and to rehydrate the body. Among island populations, coconut water, meat, and milk have been used as both food and medicine for generations. Coconut in one form or another is used to relieve digestive problems, ward off infections, speed recovery from injuries, and maintain good health.

While the coconut is highly valued for its nutritional and curative properties, it is the oil in the coconut that makes it a truly superior health food. At one time coconut oil had the misfortune of being labeled a dietary troublemaker because it is high in saturated fat. Many people avoided it for that reason. What most people didn't know at the time was that the saturated fat in coconut oil was a unique type composed predominately of medium-chain triglycerides. This fat is completely different from the saturated fat found in meats and other vegetable oils and has a number of health benefits. Ironically, one of the benefits of coconut oil is that it helps *protect* against heart disease and stroke.

This fact is clearly evident in populations around the world who rely on coconut for food and eat it every day of their lives. For thousands of years

15

people in Southeast Asia, the Philippines, Thailand, India, Sri Lanka, and elsewhere have been consuming coconuts and coconut oil without any ill effect. In these countries heart disease is relatively rare. In fact, those people who eat the most coconut have the lowest heart disease rates in the world. Even though people in the coconut growing regions of the world consume coconut oil every day of their lives, heart disease was completely unknown to them until just a few decades ago. Heart disease didn't show up until after they began replacing traditional foods, such as coconut, with Western foods. Coconut was one of the key ingredients in their diets that protected them from heart disease as well as a number of other illnesses.

Coconut oil holds a high place of respect in traditional forms of medicine throughout the world. It is highly regarded in Ayurvedic medicine of India. In coastal Africa and South and Central America, coconut oil is a folk medicine used internally and externally to treat all types of health problems. In the Caribbean coconut is considered a health tonic "good for the heart." In the coconut growing regions of South America, people have a saying: "A coconut a day keeps the doctor away." Many Polynesian populations consider it the cure for *all* illness. Among the Islanders in the South Pacific the coconut palm is so highly regarded it is revered as the "Tree of Life."

In traditional forms of medicine, coconut oil is used to treat a wide variety of health problems ranging from burns and constipation to influenza and gonorrhea. Modern medicine is now confirming many of the benefits attributed to coconut oil.

Years ago it was discovered that human breast milk contained medium-chain triglycerides. When eaten, the body transforms these triglycerides into powerful germ-fighting substances that kill disease-causing viruses, bacteria, and fungi. Researchers have determined that it is due primarily to the presence of medium-chain triglycerides in breast milk that protects infants from infections for the first few months of their lives.

The medium-chain triglycerides in coconut oil are identical to those in human breast milk and contain the same germ-fighting properties. Research has shown that these coconut oil derived substances kill microorganisms that cause sinus infections, pneumonia, bladder infections, ringworm, candidiasis, influenza, measles, herpes, mononucleosis, hepatitis C, and many other illnesses. It's no wonder coconut oil has gained a reputation in traditional medicine as a miracle cure. Because of its germ-fighting properties, medium-chain triglycerides (MCTs) derived from coconut oil are routinely added to infant formula.

In addition to the germ-fighting properties, medical research has shown that medium-chain triglycerides also possess anti-inflammatory and antioxidant properties, all of which help protect the arteries from clogging up with plaque and the heart from succumbing to heart disease. This further confirms the observation that those people who eat lots of coconut oil have a low incidence of heart disease. For those who want to learn more about the healing miracles of coconut oil I highly recommend my book *The Coconut Oil Miracle.*

Coconut oil can also help people lose excess body fat, increase energy, and improve thyroid function. Some people worry that if they add coconut oil to their diets, they will be consuming extra calories and end up gaining weight. This is not so. In fact, just the opposite happens. The fatty acids in coconut oil are used by the body as a source of fuel to produce energy. Because coconut oil is used by the body as a source of fuel, it boosts energy and stimulates metabolism. This increase in metabolism, in turn, increases the rate at which calories are consumed. So by adding coconut oil into your diet, you increase your energy level and burn off more calories. Simply adding coconut oil to a meal will lower the effective number of calories in the meal. In addition, coconut oil has slightly fewer calories than any other fat. For these reasons, coconut oil has gained a reputation as being the world's only natural, low-calorie fat. Imagine that, a low-calorie fat that can help you lose weight! This is all backed by medical research. After I wrote *The Coconut Oil Miracle,* many people reported to me their success at losing weight with coconut oil. Many of these people had tried numerous diets without success. Because of the results I was seeing, I wrote another book titled *Eat Fat, Look Thin.* This book explains how to use coconut oil to raise metabolism, improve thyroid function, and lose excess weight. Both books are completely documented with numerous references to medical studies.

RECOMMENDED AMOUNT
OF COCONUT OIL

As I mentioned, most of the health benefits attributed to coconut come from the oil. For this reason, many people try to add as much of the oil into their diets as they can. The general recommendation is between 3 and 4 tablespoons a day for most adults. This calculation is based on the amount of medium-chain triglycerides a baby receives from breast milk. The amount a baby receives is known to provide protection from illness, support good digestive function, and supply needed energy.

There is no danger of consuming too much coconut oil, except that if you're not accustomed to eating much oil, you may experience runny stools. I recommend that you add coconut oil slowly into the diet and combine it with your foods as shown in the recipes in this book. Start off limiting your coconut oil intake to 1 tablespoon per day. After a couple of weeks increase it to 2 tablespoons a day and continue in this fashion until you reach the level you feel comfortable with.

Many of those who use this book will want to prepare their foods so that they get a total of 3 to 4 tablespoons of oil in their meals during the day. As you prepare the recipes in this book, you can estimate the amount of oil you consume by how much you add to the food you eat. For example, if you add 4 tablespoons of coconut oil to a fruit smoothie, and the smoothie serves two, then you know that each serving contains 2 tablespoons of oil.

But what if you use coconut meat or milk in place of coconut oil. How much oil would you be getting? You can determine that from the following table.

Approximate Amount of Coconut Oil Contained in Various Coconut Products	
Product	Oil Content
1 cup of coconut milk	2 tablespoons
1 ounce of fresh coconut	½ tablespoon
1 cup of dried, shredded coconut	1 tablespoon

Chapter 2 provides many quick and easy ways to add coconut oil to your diet using a variety of delicious beverages. You can also increase the amount of coconut oil used in many of the recipes.

Note to Readers

I'm always looking for good coconut recipes. If you have a favorite recipe that is not found in this book and would like to share it, please send it to me and I will consider adding it to a future edition of this book. Send recipes to the Coconut Research Center, P.O. Box 25203, Colorado Springs, CO 80936.

For readers who are more familiar with the metric system of measurement, the table below may be helpful in following the recipes.

Metric Conversion

4 ½ cups	1 L		475 degrees F	245 degrees C
1 cup	250 ml		425	225
½ cup	124 ml		400	205
¼ cup	60 ml		375	190
1 tablespoon	15 ml		350	175
1 teaspoon	5 ml		325	165
½ teaspoon	3 ml		300	150
¼ teaspoon	2 ml		76	25
⅛ teaspoon	1 ml			

1 ounce	28 g
16 ounces	450 g
1 pound	450 g
2.24 pounds	1 kg

Terms Used in this Book

Unless otherwise noted, the term "flour" used in the recipes of this book refers to **whole wheat flour**. All dried coconut used in these recipes is **unsweetened** and the coconut milk is **unsweetened.** The term "sugar" means any dry sweetener. "Honey" means any wet sweetener.

CHAPTER 2

Beverages

HOMEMADE COCONUT MILK AND CREAM

Commercially produced coconut milk, and to a lesser extent coconut cream, are readily available at most grocery stores. This is by far the easiest way to get these products, but if you would like to try making the milk or cream at home from a fresh coconut, this recipe will guide you through the process.

Fresh coconut milk, when refrigerated, and canned coconut milk, if not shaken, separates into two layers with the thick upper layer being the coconut cream and the thinner bottom layer the milk. The top layer can be skimmed off with a spoon and used for recipes requiring coconut cream and the bottom layer reserved for recipes specifying coconut milk.

You can get about a quart of coconut milk from a single medium-size coconut. Drain the water out of the coconut and put the liquid aside. Remove the coconut meat. You do not need to peel the brown membrane from the flesh. Put the meat and 2 cups of hot water into a blender and blend until the coconut is completely chopped. If you want the milk to be slightly sweet, use the coconut water you reserved from the coconut and reduce the amount of added water so that you have a total of 2 cups.

Over a bowl, press the contents of the blender through a double thickness of cheesecloth or a fine sieve, forcing out as much liquid as possible. This liquid is the coconut cream and is very rich. The coconut pulp still contains a lot of juice that can still be extracted. Put the pulp in a saucepan with 2 cups of water. Bring to a boil and simmer for 5 minutes. Let cool. Run it through the blender a second time. Press juice out of the pulp using cheesecloth or a sieve. Discard pulp or save it and use in other recipes to increase fiber content. Since the liquid from the second pressing will be less creamy than the first, you can mix the two together.

If you want a completely *raw* coconut milk, omit the step where you simmer the pulp in hot water. Run the pulp through the blender a second time and press the juice out as described.

If you do not use the cream or milk immediately, store it in an airtight container in the refrigerator. Use within two to three days. The cream and oil will separate out as it sits, so stir or shake well before using. The milk may need to be warmed to above 76 degrees to completely dissolve the solids.

Another way you can make an unheated coconut milk or cream is to use a juicer. Juicing fresh coconut produces a rich coconut cream. This is by far the easiest way to make coconut cream. To turn the cream into milk just dilute with a little water. Most juicers on the market, however, will not juice fresh coconut. Coconut meat is too hard on them. I know of only one juicer that can do the job and that is the Green Star Juicer. The Green Star Juicer has a powerful motor with heavy duty twin gears that crush and pulverize the coconut. The cream is separated from the pulp with ease. The cream you get from this juicer is superior to any other and far better than the canned products you buy at the store. Since you make it yourself you know it has no additives or fillers. Fresh coconut cream straight from the coconut is absolutely delicious!

SWEETENED COCONUT MILK
(An excellent replacement for cow's milk)
Fresh and canned coconut milks are naturally unsweetened, which makes them good for making soups and sauces where sweetness is not desired. Although many people enjoy drinking unsweetened coconut milk, most prefer a thinner, sweeter beverage that more closely resembles cow's milk. This recipe produces an excellent non-dairy replacement for cow's milk that can be enjoyed by the glass, poured over hot or cold cereal, or combined in a bowl with freshly cut fruit. This recipe makes about 2 ¾ cups of milk. Coconut milk spoils quickly, so keep it refrigerated and use within three or four days.

1 can (14 ounces) coconut milk
1 cup water
2 tablespoons honey
Dash of salt

Mix all ingredients together. For sweeter milk add more honey. For creamier milk use less water. Put in an airtight container and store in the refrigerator. Serve chilled.

Variations
Adding 1 tablespoon of imitation coconut extract, vanilla, or almond extract can enhance the flavor of the Sweetened Coconut Milk. These flavors give

the milk a wonderful added taste. Makes a great base for the Fresh Fruit Flavored Milks described below.

COCONUT WATER

Coconut water is the liquid that forms inside the coconut. Unlike coconut milk, which is made from expelling the liquid from coconut meat, coconut water is naturally sweet. The taste of coconut water varies somewhat according to the age of the coconut. The water from a fresh green (immature) coconut is very sweet and tasteful. It has a delicious flavor I would describe as similar to caramel. The water from mature coconuts isn't nearly as flavorful. Because of its sweetness, it can be used to sweeten other beverages such as fruit smoothies and blender drinks. Unfortunately, unless you live where coconuts are grown, it is difficult to get green coconuts. However, coconut water from green coconuts is now being commercially packaged in bottles and tetra paks and is available in many stores.

Coconut Milk and Water Mix ❤

½ cup coconut milk
½ cup coconut water

Combining equal portions of coconut water and milk makes a deliciously coconutty flavored, slightly sweet, beverage. It is excellent for use on hot or cold breakfast cereal, over fruit, or by the glass. It is a very healthy alternative to cow's milk. Use water from a fresh green coconut or a commercially packaged product for best results.

CREAMY COCONUT BEVERAGES

The following beverages use coconut milk as a base. Coconut cream may also be used if you desire a richer flavor and thicker consistency.

FRESH FRUIT FLAVORED MILKS

The following recipes use the Sweetened Coconut Milk or Coconut Milk and Water Mix as a base in combination with fruits and flavorings to produce a variety of flavored milks. These milks taste great by the glass and can be used over hot or cold cereal.

Strawberry Milk ♥
1 cup Sweetened Coconut Milk
1 cup strawberries, sliced

Mix Sweetened Coconut Milk and strawberries in a blender. Chill and serve.

Banana Milk
1 cup Sweetened Coconut Milk
1 ripe banana, sliced

Mix Sweetened Coconut Milk and banana in a blender. Chill and serve.

Mango Milk
1 cup Sweetened Coconut Milk
1 mango, chopped

Mix Sweetened Coconut Milk and mango in a blender. Chill and serve.

Blueberry Milk
1 cup Sweetened Coconut Milk
1 cup ripe blueberries

Mix Sweetened Coconut Milk and blueberries in a blender. Chill and serve.

Apricot Milk
1 cup Sweetened Coconut Milk
1 cup apricots, chopped

Mix Sweetened Coconut Milk and apricots in a blender. Chill and serve.

Kiwi Milk
1 cup Sweetened Coconut Milk
2 kiwis, peeled

Mix Sweetened Coconut Milk and kiwis in a blender. Chill and serve.

Pineapple Milk
1 cup Sweetened Coconut Milk
1 cup pineapple, chopped

Mix Sweetened Coconut Milk and pineapple in a blender. Chill and serve.

Pineapple Banana Milk
1 cup Sweetened Coconut Milk
½ cup pineapple, chopped
½ banana, sliced

Mix Sweetened Coconut Milk, pineapple, and banana in a blender. Chill and serve.

PINA COLADA FRUIT DRINK
This drink can be made from freshly squeezed juices or from frozen concentrate.

¾ cup orange juice
¼ cup pineapple juice
¼ cup coconut milk

Combine ingredients and mix thoroughly. Serve chilled.

CREAMY FRUIT PUNCH
You can transform most any fruit juice into a creamy delight with this simple recipe.

¼ cup coconut milk
1 cup fruit juice

Mix coconut milk and prepared fruit juice together. Chill and serve. You can use most any flavor of fruit juice available at your grocery store.

HOT CHOCOLATE
This is a great tasting dairy-free chocolate drink.

2 tablespoons cocoa
¼ cup sugar
Dash of salt
3 tablespoons water

1¾ cup coconut milk
1 teaspoon vanilla

Mix cocoa, sugar, and salt in saucepan; stir in water. Cook and stir over medium heat until mixture boils; boil and stir 2 minutes. Stir in coconut milk and heat. Do not boil. Remove from heat and add vanilla. Serve hot.

CHOCOLATE ALMOND ♥

2 tablespoons cocoa
¼ cup sugar
Dash of salt
3 tablespoons water
1¾ cup coconut milk
1 teaspoon vanilla
1 teaspoon almond extract

Mix cocoa, sugar, and salt in saucepan; stir in water. Cook and stir over medium heat until mixture boils; boil and stir 2 minutes. Stir in coconut milk and cook until hot, but do not boil. Remove from heat and add vanilla and almond extract. Serve hot or cold.

CHOCOLATE MINT

2 tablespoons cocoa
¼ cup sugar
Dash of salt
3 tablespoons water
1¾ cup coconut milk
1 teaspoon vanilla
½ teaspoon peppermint extract

Mix cocoa, sugar, and salt in saucepan; stir in water. Cook and stir over medium heat until mixture boils; boil and stir 2 minutes. Stir in coconut milk and heat. Do not boil. Remove from heat and add vanilla and peppermint extract. Serve hot or cold

ORANGE CREAM ♥

¾ cup orange juice
¼ cup coconut milk

Mix orange juice and coconut milk together. Produces a delightfully creamy orange drink. Serve chilled.

EGGNOG

¼ cup water
1 ½ tablespoons sugar
1 teaspoon nutmeg
1 can (14 ounces) coconut milk
1 egg
Dash of salt
1 tablespoon vanilla
½ teaspoon almond extract

Put water and sugar in a saucepan and heat to boiling. Stir nutmeg into hot water, remove from heat and let cool for 1 minute. Combine water with coconut milk in a mixing bowl. Add all remaining ingredients and mix thoroughly with electric beater or blender. Chill and serve.

CINNAMON EGGNOG

¼ cup water
1 ½ tablespoons sugar
1 teaspoon cinnamon
¼ teaspoon nutmeg
1 can (4 ounces) coconut milk
1 egg
Dash of salt
1 tablespoon vanilla
½ teaspoon almond extract

Put water and sugar in a saucepan and heat to boiling. Stir cinnamon and nutmeg into hot water, remove from heat and let cool for 1 minute. Combine water with coconut milk in a mixing bowl. Add all remaining ingredients and mix thoroughly with electric beater or blender. Chill and serve.

VANILLA CREAM

¼ cup water
1½ tablespoons brown sugar or maple syrup
1 can (14 ounces) coconut milk
Dash of salt
1 tablespoon vanilla
1 egg (optional)

Combine all ingredients in a mixing bowl and mix thoroughly with electric beater or blender. Chill and serve.

PEPPERMINT CREAM

¼ cup water
1½ tablespoons sugar
1 can (14 ounces) coconut milk
Dash of salt
1 tablespoon vanilla
½ teaspoon peppermint extract
1 egg (optional)

Combine all ingredients in a mixing bowl and mix thoroughly with electric beater or blender. Chill and serve.

VEGETABLE DRINKS

Coconut milk naturally goes well with fruit drinks. Vegetable drinks, however, aren't as compatible. The following drinks do not use coconut milk but do include coconut oil. These drinks serve as a convenient way to add health promoting coconut oil to the diet without adding sugar or sweet fruits.

TOMATO JUICE COCKTAIL ♥

This drink is good served hot and tastes much like a light tomato soup. Goes well with coconut oil, making a convenient way of adding the oil into the diet.

1 can (8 ounces) tomato sauce
1 ½ cups water
¼ teaspoon onion powder
1 ½ teaspoons lemon juice
2 tablespoons coconut oil
¼ teaspoon salt
Pepper to taste

Combine tomato sauce, water, and onion powder in a small saucepan. Heat until hot. Remove from heat and stir in lemon juice and coconut oil. Add salt and pepper to taste. Stir and enjoy.

SNAPPY TOMATO JUICE COCKTAIL

This is a spiced up version of the Tomato Juice Cocktail. It has a little more flavor and a bit of a kick.

1 can (8 ounces) tomato sauce
1 ½ cups water
½ teaspoon onion powder
Dash or two of cayenne pepper
¼ teaspoon garlic powder
¼ teaspoon paprika
1 ½ teaspoons lemon juice
2 tablespoons coconut oil
¼ teaspoon salt
Pepper to taste

Combine tomato sauce, water, onion powder, cayenne pepper, garlic powder, and paprika in a small saucepan. Heat to boiling, reduce heat and simmer 1 minute. Remove from heat and stir in lemon juice and coconut oil. Add salt and pepper. Stir and enjoy.

TEX-MEX TOMATO JUICE CACKTAIL
This spicy drink has a bit of a kick to it.

½ cup tomato sauce
½ cup salsa
1 ½ cups water
¼ teaspoon chili powder
1 teaspoon lemon juice
2 tablespoons coconut oil
¼ teaspoon salt
Pepper to taste

Combine tomato sauce, salsa, water, and chili powder in a small saucepan. Heat just to boiling, remove from burner, and stir in lemon juice and coconut oil. Add salt and pepper. Stir and enjoy.

SHRIMP COCKTAIL DRINK ♥

1 ½ cups water
½ cup shrimp, cooked
½ teaspoon onion powder
1 can (8 ounces) tomato sauce
1 teaspoon lemon juice
1 teaspoon cilantro
2 tablespoons coconut oil
Salt and pepper to taste

Combine water, shrimp, and onion powder in a small saucepan. Heat until hot and simmer for 1 minute. Remove from heat, add tomato sauce, lemon juice, cilantro, and blend in blender. Stir in coconut oil, salt, and pepper. Serve warm.

SMOOTHIES AND BLENDER DRINKS

There are as many smoothie recipes as there are people who make them. The combinations are nearly endless. There are no rules for making smoothies, and virtually any combination of fruits can produce a decent tasting beverage.

30

Experimenting with different ingredients adds variety and adventure to the experience. Fruit smoothies are generally made with a liquid base such as milk or fruit juice with some combination of fresh or frozen fruits. Vegetables, vitamin and mineral supplements, wheat bran, seeds and nuts, and a variety of other ingredients are often added for their nutritional or health properties.

The liquid you use as a base for your smoothie can be milk, juice, or, my favorite, coconut milk or coconut cream. Another liquid you can use is coconut water. Being naturally sweet, coconut water will sweeten up any smoothie, eliminating the need for added sweeteners.

Because fruit is a primary ingredient, most smoothies are sweet. The level of sweetness depends on the ingredients you use and your taste. Some smoothies have added sweeteners while others rely only on the fruits or juice for sweetness. When sour (or unripe) fruits, unsweetened yogurt, or other ingredients are used, the smoothie often needs a little sweetening. You can use any sweetener of your choice, including stevia. If you don't like to use processed sweeteners, you can add apple or grape juice, well ripened bananas, pineapple, raisins, or dates.

Raisins make a nice natural sweetener. But you can't just add them in the blender because they don't chop up finely enough. In order for the raisins to blend well, they need to be softened first. Heat 1 cup of water in a saucepan to boiling, remove from heat, and add ¼ to ½ cup raisins. Soak the raisins for 1 hour. Another method is to soak the raisins in cool water for several hours or overnight. Blend the softened raisins with about 1 cup of liquid before adding any of the other ingredients. Once the raisins are chopped, add the remaining ingredients.

Smoothies can be very liquidy or as thick as milkshakes. I recommend you use cold ingredients (except for the coconut oil and egg mixture described in Super Healthy Blender Drinks below). For a thick smoothie, peel and cut the fruit beforehand and put it in the freezer. Blend frozen fruit with cold juice, yogurt, or coconut milk. Coconut milk tends to thicken somewhat when chilled and makes a great thick smoothie. If your smoothie is too runny, pop it into the freezer for an hour or two. If it freezes too much, put it back into the blender. It will come out perfect.

The following recipes are just a few of the many smoothies you can make. Experiment by using different types of fruits and different combinations. Yogurt can add a delightful, creamy tartness to smoothies. You can use plain or flavored yogurt, whichever suits your taste. I like the plain as well as the vanilla and maple flavored yogurts because they combine well with just about any type of fruit.

BASIC COCONUT MILK SMOOTHIE ♥

1 large ripe banana
1 cup coconut milk
1 cup orange juice

Blend all ingredients in blender until smooth. This smoothie recipe can be used as the base for many different flavors. (Coconut oil can be added if desired; follow directions as described on pages 36-37.)

Fruit Coconut Milk Smoothie
Make the Basic Coconut Milk Smoothie above and add 1 to 2 cups of any of the following fruits: raspberries, blackberries, boysenberries, tart cherries, pineapple, peaches, apricots, mango, papaya, strawberries, kiwi, or nectarines.

TROPICAL FRUIT SMOOTHIE

1 cup mango, sliced
1 cup pineapple, chopped
1 ripe banana
Juice of 1 fresh lime
1 cup coconut milk
4 ice cubes

Chill all fruit and coconut milk before starting. Place all ingredients into blender and blend until smooth.

ZESTY PEACH SMOOTHIE

2 ripe peaches, pitted and peeled
¾ cup orange juice
½ cup coconut milk

½ teaspoon ground cinnamon
⅛ teaspoon ground ginger

Chill liquids and peaches before starting. Peaches can be prepared beforehand and frozen if desired. Place all ingredients into blender and blend until smooth.

YOGURT SMOOTHIE ♥

¼ to ½ cup raisins, soaked, or use other sweetener
1 cup orange juice
1 cup coconut milk
1 cup plain yogurt
1 banana

Soak raisins at least 1 hour in hot water or in cool water overnight. Mix in the blender with 1 cup of orange juice until the raisins are pulverized. Add remaining ingredients and blend until smooth. Serves two.

CHERRY YOGURT SMOOTHIE

1 cup coconut milk
½ cup plain yogurt
1 ripe banana
2 cups cherries, pitted
⅛ teaspoon almond extract
4 ice cubes
2 tablespoons grated coconut (optional)

Chill all ingredients before using. Combine in a blender and blend until smooth. For added fiber you can add grated coconut.

CHOCOLATE FRUIT SMOOTHIE
This is a thick, rich flavored drink that, when frozen, tastes a lot like ice cream.

2 ripe bananas, chopped and frozen
1 cup strawberries, sliced and frozen

33

¼ cup water
1 ½ tablespoons sugar or sweetener of your choice
¼ cup cocoa
Dash of salt
1 cup coconut milk
¼ teaspoon vanilla

Peel, slice, and freeze banana and strawberries overnight. Heat water, sugar, cocoa, and salt in saucepan. Bring to a boil, stirring constantly, reduce heat and simmer for 2 minutes. Stir in coconut milk. Remove from heat, add vanilla, cool, and place in refrigerator until chilled. Combine chocolate mixture, frozen bananas, and frozen strawberries in a blender and blend together until smooth. For a thinner smoothie add a little more water.

Chocolate Peanut Butter Smoothie
Make Chocolate Fruit Smoothie as directed but omit the strawberries and add ¼ cup peanut butter. Almond butter can be used in place of peanut butter if desired.

PINA COLADA SMOOTHIE
This drink uses coconut water.

1 cup coconut milk
1 cup coconut water
1 cup pineapple
1 banana

Chill ingredients, including the banana, before using. Combine in a blender and blend until smooth.

CITRUS REFRESHER
This drink is made with coconut water.

1 cup coconut milk
1 cup coconut water
1 banana
1 ½ cups orange juice (or 2 fresh oranges)
¼ cup lime juice (juice from 2 fresh limes)

Chill ingredients, including the banana, before using. Combine in a blender and blend until smooth.

CREAMY PEACH
This beverage uses coconut water.
1 cup coconut milk
1 cup coconut water
4 peaches, pitted and peeled
¼ teaspoon almond extract
¼ cup almonds (optional)

Chill peaches, coconut milk, and coconut water before using. Combine all ingredients in a blender and blend until smooth.

SUPER HEALTHY BLENDER DRINKS

Smoothies and blender drinks made from fresh fruits and vegetables provides a good source of vitamins, minerals, and fiber. When coconut oil is added, the nutritional value greatly increases. Coconut oil provides many health benefits. It aids the body in fighting off infections, improves digestive function, and increases metabolism and energy level. In order to experience noticeable improvement in health and well-being, nutritionists usually recommend that adults get from 2 to 4 tablespoons of coconut oil a day. Some doctors recommended up to 6 tablespoons a day for their sick patients.

One cup of coconut milk or coconut cream contains approximately 2 tablespoons of coconut oil. So if you use 1 cup of coconut milk in your smoothie, you will get the equivalent of 2 tablespoons of coconut oil.

If you want to increase the oil content of a smoothie without adding more coconut milk, you can. Simply mix the coconut milk and oil together in the blender *before* adding any other ingredients. This works best if the coconut milk is at room temperature and the oil is melted. As much as 2 tablespoons of coconut oil can be easily blended into 1 cup of coconut milk. Combing the milk and oil will produce a cup of coconut milk with the equivalent of 4 tablespoons of oil.

When you add coconut oil to a smoothie, it *must* be mixed with coconut milk first. The other ingredients are added afterwards. The problem with adding coconut oil later is that the oil solidifies at temperatures below 76 degrees F. This explains why coconut oil sitting in a jar in your kitchen can be liquid one day and solid the next. If the temperature in your kitchen is over 76 degrees F, the oil will be liquid. If you add melted coconut oil to a cold smoothie consisting of ingredients right out of the refrigerator or freezer, the oil will harden as soon as it hits the mixture. The blender will not blend the oil but will chop it into little chunks or beads, which many people find unappetizing.

Another problem with adding coconut oil to smoothies, and especially blender drinks and juices, is that oil and water don't mix. The oil separates and floats to the top. This problem is easily solved if you add an emulsifier. Coconut milk can emulsify the oil if mixed together separately, as described above. However, sometimes you may want to add coconut oil to a smoothie or drink that does not contain coconut milk. What do you use as an emulsifier? Egg yolk serves this purpose very well.

I prefer to use whole *raw* eggs. If you use organic eggs, there is virtually no risk of salmonella contamination. If you are squeamish about eating raw eggs, hard boil the egg first then remove the shell and egg white. Put the cooked *egg yolk* in the blender with the oil. You can blend at least 6 tablespoons of oil with 1 egg. I generally use 4 tablespoons (¼ cup) in a smoothie that serves two (about 1 quart). After the egg and oil are thoroughly mixed, add the rest of the ingredients and make the smoothie as you normally would. The oil will be completely blended into the smoothie and undetectable. The egg and oil blend best if the egg is warmed to about room temperature. After the oil has been emulsified in the egg, cold and frozen ingredients can be added without problem.

You can use the same method to combine coconut oil with blender drinks and fruit and vegetable juices. This makes a very easy and tasty way to get your daily recommended dose of coconut oil. You can combine 1, 2, 3, or more tablespoons of oil into any type of juice or beverage by emulsifying it first with an egg.

Raw eggs supply the highest quality protein available in our diet and are packed with vitamins and minerals. If desired, you can also add dietary supplements, fiber, herbs, and other products to boost the nutritional value of the smoothie. Coconut oil combined with fruit, vegetables, eggs, and a variety of supplements makes a super healthy blender drink.

MANGO SMOOTHIE

1 cup coconut milk
2 tablespoons coconut oil
1 cup orange juice
1 fresh mango, peeled and pitted

Blend coconut milk and melted oil together in blender. Add orange juice and mango and blend until smooth.

PINEAPPLE SMOOTHIE

1 cup coconut milk
2 tablespoons coconut oil
1 cup orange juice
1 cup fresh pineapple
1 banana

Blend coconut milk and melted oil together in blender. Add remaining ingredients and blend until smooth.

COCONUT OIL JUICE MIX
This is a basic recipe that will work with any type of fruit or vegetable juice.

1 raw egg
1 to 6 tablespoons coconut oil, melted but not hot
1 to 2 cups juice of your choice

Warm the egg to about room temperature. You can do this quickly by immersing egg in a cup of hot tap water for a minute or two. Mix egg and melted oil together in a blender for about 10 seconds (1 cooked egg yolk can be substituted for the raw egg if you prefer). Add cold or even warm juice, if you like, and blend together for a few seconds. It's ready to drink and enjoy. If desired, you can add vitamins and other supplements to turn this drink into a nutritional powerhouse.

PEACH YOGURT SMOOTHIE

¼ cup raisins, soaked
1 raw egg
¼ cup coconut oil
1 cup orange juice
3 to 4 peaches, peeled, pitted, and sliced
1 cup yogurt (plain, vanilla, or maple)

Soak raisins at least 1 hour in hot water or in cool water overnight. For a sweeter smoothie, use more raisins. Combine egg with coconut oil in blender and mix until well blended (about 10 seconds). Add raisins and orange juice. Blend until raisins are pulverized. Add remaining ingredients and blend until smooth. Serves two.

STRAWBERRY BANANA SMOOTHIE

1 raw egg
¼ cup coconut oil
1 cup yogurt (plain, vanilla, or maple)
2 cups strawberries
1 banana
1 cup pineapple

Combine egg with coconut oil in blender and mix until well blended (about 10 seconds). Add remaining ingredients and blend until smooth. Serves two.

POWERHOUSE MANGO MILK

This is a novel substitute for dairy milk. It is nearly white in appearance and somewhat resembles milk. It has a mildly sweet, coconutty fruit flavor. You can use it in place of milk on cold or hot cereal, drink it by the glass, use as liquid base for smoothies, serve in a bowl with fresh fruit, etc.

1 raw egg
1 to 6 tablespoons coconut oil
3 cups mango juice
1 cup cold water

Mix egg and coconut oil in a blender. You can use up to 6 tablespoons of coconut oil, but 2 to 4 are usually enough. Add mango juice and water and blend together. You can use fresh or frozen juice. Any type of commercial mango juice or juice combination will work, such as mango peach or mango orange. If mango isn't available, you can also get good results with peach or apricot juices.

V-8 JUICE BLEND

¼ cup coconut oil
1 raw egg
2 cups V-8 Juice

Blend coconut oil and raw egg (or cooked egg yolk) in blender. Add V-8 Juice or a vegetable juice blend made with your own juicer.

CHAPTER 3

Salads

SALAD DRESSINGS

COCONUT MAYONNAISE

Coconut mayonnaise made with 100 percent coconut oil tends to harden when refrigerated and so can only be used when freshly made. This recipe can be made ahead of time, stored in the refrigerator, and still remain soft and spreadable. The secret to this mayonnaise is the addition of a little olive oil. If you don't mind your mayonnaise tasting like olive oil you can use extra virgin olive oil. If you prefer a more traditional or mild tasting mayonnaise, I suggest you use a mild flavored olive oil.

2 egg yolks
2 tablespoons lemon juice
½ tablespoon prepared mustard, preferably Dijon-style
⅛ teaspoon paprika
⅛ teaspoon salt
¼ cup olive oil
1 cup coconut oil

Combine egg yolks, lemon juice, mustard, paprika, salt, and olive oil in blender or food processor. Blend for about 60 seconds. While machine is running, pour in coconut oil *very* slowly in a fine steady stream. The secret to making good mayonnaise is to add the oil *slowly*. Mayonnaise will thicken as oil is added. Taste and adjust seasoning as needed.

THOUSAND ISLAND DRESSING

½ cup Coconut Mayonnaise
2 tablespoons chili sauce or ketchup
¼ cup pickle relish
⅛ teaspoon paprika
Salt and pepper to taste

Mix all ingredients together in bowl. Store in airtight container in refrigerator. Remains soft when chilled.

BUTTERMILK DRESSING

¾ cup Coconut Mayonnaise (page 41)
½ cup buttermilk
1 teaspoon dried dill
½ teaspoon instant minced onion
¼ teaspoon garlic powder
½ teaspoon salt
Dash of pepper

Blend all ingredients together. Put in refrigerator and let sit for at least 1 hour.

VINAIGRETTE

¼ cup extra virgin olive oil
¼ cup coconut oil
¼ cup vinegar
3 tablespoons water
½ teaspoon onion powder
½ teaspoon dill
½ teaspoon salt
⅛ teaspoon pepper

Put all ingredients into a screw-top jar. Cover and shake vigorously until well blended. Let it sit at room temperature for 1 hour. Store in the refrigerator.

ITALIAN DRESSING ♥

¼ cup extra virgin olive oil
¼ cup coconut oil
¼ cup apple cider vinegar
3 tablespoons water
1 envelope (.7-ounce) Good Seasons Italian Dressing mix

Put all ingredients into a screw-top jar. Cover and shake well. Let it sit at room temperature for 1 hour. Store in the refrigerator.

CREAMY COCONUT DRESSING ♥

This dressing is great for fruit salads or fruit and vegetable salad combinations. It has a mild sweetness that enhances the natural sweetness of fresh fruits and vegetables. Any of the four "C" Dressings (Coconut, Cinnamon, Cardamom, and Curry) can be used interchangeably in the recipes that follow.

1 cup coconut milk
1 tablespoon cornstarch
½ tablespoon honey
Dash of salt

In a saucepan, mix coconut milk and cornstarch together until blended. Add honey and salt, cook at low to moderate heat, stirring constantly, until mixture thickens and all taste of cornstarch is gone (about 5 minutes). Remove from heat and let cool. Mix with salad and chill. Dressing can be made ahead of time and stored in the refrigerator until ready to use.

Creamy Cinnamon Dressing

Make Creamy Coconut Dressing as directed and add 1 teaspoon cinnamon with the cornstarch. This makes a great-tasting dressing for fruit salads.

Creamy Cardamom Dressing

Make Creamy Coconut Dressing as directed and add 1 teaspoon cardamom with the cornstarch. This dressing adds a unique flavor to salads.

Creamy Curry Dressing

Make Creamy Coconut Dressing as directed and add 1 teaspoon curry powder with the cornstarch. This mildly spicy dressing adds a pleasant kick to fruit and vegetable salads.

MANGO DRESSING

This dressing is a spicy blend of sweet and sour that goes well with both fruit and vegetable salads.

1 mango, chopped
½ cup coconut milk
2 tablespoons rice vinegar or 1 tablespoon white wine vinegar
2 tablespoons of fresh lime juice

1 teaspoon paprika
1 tablespoon sucanat or honey
⅛ teaspoon salt
Dash of cayenne pepper

Puree all ingredients in blender until smooth. Season to taste with salt. Chill.

SESAME SEED DRESSING ❤

This is an excellent dressing for tossed green salads.

½ cup coconut oil
¼ cup sesame seeds
¼ cup slivered almonds
1 tablespoon olive oil
2 tablespoons tamari sauce
1 tablespoon apple cider vinegar
¼ teaspoon ground ginger
¼ teaspoon salt

Put coconut oil in a small saucepan. At medium to low heat sauté sesame seeds and slivered almonds until lightly brown. Remove from heat and let cool to room temperature. Stir in remaining ingredients. As the dressing sits, the oil will separate to the top and the sesame seeds and almonds will sink to the bottom. Stir just before using. Spoon dressing onto salad making sure to include the sesame seeds and almonds.

SALADS

WALDORF SALAD ❤

2 medium apples, diced
2 medium stalks celery, chopped
½ cup coarsely chopped nuts (walnuts or pecans)
Creamy Coconut Dressing (page 43)

Stir all ingredients together, adding just enough dressing for good consistency. Stir well and serve on a bed of lettuce leaves. Creamy Cinnamon, Cardamom, or Curry Dressing could be used with this salad if desired.

AMBROSIA ❤

1 cup pineapple chunks
1 can (11 ounces) mandarin orange segments, drained
1 medium apple, chopped
2 medium bananas, sliced
¼ cup raisins
1 cup coarsely chopped pecans
½ cup coconut flakes
Creamy Coconut Dressing (page 43)

Stir all ingredients together. Add enough dressing for good consistency. Serve chilled on a bed of lettuce leaves.

BANANA COCONUT SALAD

This is a very simple, easy-to-make salad.

2 large bananas
¼ cup shredded coconut, toasted

Peel and slice the bananas. Toast coconut in 350 degree F oven for about 10 minutes or until lightly brown. Mix coconut and banana slices together. Serve fresh.

TROPICAL ISLAND SALAD

1 cup pineapple, chopped
1 banana, sliced
1 orange, sectioned and cut-up
1 mango, sliced into bite-size pieces
½ cup coconut, shredded
Creamy Coconut Dressing (page 43)
Mixed salad greens
Toasted flaked coconut

Combine the first five ingredients together and add just enough dressing for good consistency. Stir well and serve on a bed of mixed salad greens. Garnish with toasted flaked coconut.

RASPBERRY BANANA SALAD

1 envelope raspberry or cherry flavored Jello
2 cups Fruit Sauce made with raspberries (page 56)
1 large banana, sliced

Make Jello according to package directions. Put into the refrigerator for about 45 minutes until partially set but still pourable. Fold in Fruit Sauce. Layer banana slices on top of Jello mixture. Chill until firm, about 3 to 5 hours. Serve on a bed of lettuce.

CREAMY MELON

2 cups watermelon, chopped
2 cups cantaloupe, chopped
1 orange, sectioned
½ cup blueberries
Creamy Coconut Dressing (page 43)
Toasted flaked coconut (optional)

Stir all ingredients together. Serve chilled with Creamy Coconut Dressing. If desired top with toasted flaked coconut.

ORANGE BANANA

1 orange, segmented
1 banana, sliced
Creamy Coconut Dressing (page 43)
Mixed greens
¼ cup shredded or flaked coconut, toasted

Mix orange, banana, and Creamy Coconut Dressing together. Place on bed of mixed greens and top with toasted coconut.

CANTALOUPE CHERRY SALAD

½ cantaloupe, cut into balls or cubes
1 cup dark sweet cherries, pitted
1 cup green grapes
Creamy Coconut Dressing (page 43)

Mix fruit together and add enough dressing for good consistency. Serve chilled.

SUMMER FRUIT SALAD

1 cup strawberries, cut into halves
½ cup seedless grapes, cut into halves
2 medium peaches
2 small bananas

Mix fruit together and add enough dressing for good consistency. Serve chilled on a bed of lettuce leaves.

PEACH SALAD

2 peaches, cut into bite-size pieces
1 cup pineapple, chopped
2 cups mixed salad greens
Creamy Cinnamon Dressing (page 43)

Combine peaches and pineapple. Add enough dressing to generously coat the fruit. Serve chilled on a bed of mixed salad greens.

APPLE CINNAMON SALAD

2 apples, chopped
¼ cup raisins
Creamy Cinnamon Dressing (page 43)
Sliced almonds, toasted

Mix apples and raisins together with Creamy Cinnamon Dressing and chill. Spread almonds in a single layer on baking dish or cookie sheet; bake at 325 degrees F or about 10 minutes or until lightly browned, let cool. Sprinkle almonds on top of salad just before serving.

CARROT APPLE CURRY

2 carrots, shredded
1 apple, diced
¼ cup raisins
¼ cup nuts
Creamy Curry Dressing (page 43)

Combine all ingredients, adding just enough dressing for good consistency. Serve chilled.

ZESTY MANGO BANANA

1 mango, chopped
1 banana, sliced
1 orange, sectioned
Curry or Mango Dressing (page 43)

Combine fruit. Serve chilled with Curry or Mango Dressing.

TOSSED CURRY SALAD

2 cups mixed salad greens
½ cucumber, sliced
½ half green pepper, chopped
3 scallions, chopped
1 peach, cut into bite-size pieces
Curry or Mango Dressing (page 43)
¼ cup toasted cashews

Toss first five ingredients together and chill. Serve with Curry or Mango Dressing topped with cashews.

PINEAPPLE CURRY

1 cup pineapple, chopped
1 banana, sliced
¼ cup roasted peanuts
Curry Dressing (page 43)

Toss all ingredients together, serve chilled with Curry or Mango Dressing.

PEACH CURRY

2 peaches, cut-up
1 banana, sliced
¼ cup roasted peanuts or almonds
Curry Dressing (page 43)

Toss all ingredients together, serve chilled with Curry or Mango Dressing.

PEANUT BUTTER APPLE SLAW

2 cups cabbage, shredded
1 cup fresh pineapple, cubed
1 apple, chopped
¼ cup shredded coconut
½ cup peanut butter
½ cup Creamy Coconut Dressing (page 43)
Dash of salt

Combine first four ingredients. In a separate bowl mix peanut butter with Creamy Coconut Dressing and a dash of salt. Combine ingredients and serve chilled.

JICAMA MANGO SALAD

1 cup jicama, shredded
4 scallions, chopped

*4 cups romaine lettuce, in bite-size pieces, or 1 10-ounce bag mixed baby
  lettuce
¾ cup roasted cashews
½ cup shredded or flaked coconut
1 mango, chopped*
1 can (11 ounces) Mandarin oranges, drained
Mango Dressing (page 43)*

Mix all ingredients together and keep chilled. Add Mango Dressing just before serving.

*You may use a peach in place of the mango if desired.

POTATO SALAD

*6 medium red potatoes, cubed
1 cup Coconut Mayonnaise (page 41)
1 tablespoon prepared mustard*

¼ cup apple cider vinegar
½ medium bell pepper, chopped
½ cup scallions, sliced
2 stalks celery, diced
½ cup chopped dill pickle
1½ teaspoons salt
⅛ teaspoon pepper

Boil potatoes until tender, but still firm. Set aside to cool. Stir all ingredients together and serve. If desired, a sliced hard boiled egg can be added as a garnish.

Herbed Potato Salad
Make Potato Salad as directed but add ¼ teaspoon dried marjoram and 1 teaspoon dried dill.

SESAME CHICKEN SALAD ♥
This salad is so hearty and tasty it should be eaten as a main dish.

1 cup cooked chicken, cut in bite-size pieces
4 to 6 cups mixed lettuce
4 scallions, sliced
1 tomato, chopped
1 bell pepper, chopped
6 to 12 fried wonton skins or wrappers (page 87)*
Sesame Seed Dressing (page 44)

Mix vegetables and chicken together in a bowl. Serve in individual bowls and add Sesame Seed Dressing as desired. Break fried wonton skins into bite-sized pieces and sprinkle on top of salad as a garnish.

*You may substitute 1 cup of toasted flaked coconut for the wonton if you desire. To toast coconut, place in oven at 350 degrees F for 8 to 10 minutes or until golden brown.

JAPANESE VEGETABLE SALAD
WITH SESAME SEED DRESSING

2 cups mixed salad greens
1 cup red cabbage, shredded or finely cut
1 cup cucumber, shredded
½ cup radishes, shredded
½ cup carrot, shredded
½ cup cooked shrimp, minced
Sesame Seed Dressing (page 44)

Place greens, vegetables, and shrimp in a large salad bowl. Pour Sesame Seed Dressing into bowl and toss well to mix.

TURKEY CALYPSO SALAD

½ cup brown rice
¼ cup wild rice
1 cup flaked coconut
½ red bell pepper, chopped
1 tablespoon chili pepper, finely diced
5 scallions, chopped
1 rib celery, chopped
1 tablespoon cilantro
2 mangos or peaches, chopped
¼ to ½ pound turkey or chicken, cut into matchstick strips
Orange Dressing (below)

Cook brown rice and wild rice together in 1½ cups of salted water for 50 to 60 minutes or until tender. Drain, if necessary, and cool. Heat oven to 375 degrees F. Spread coconut evenly on a baking pan. Bake in oven until lightly browned (about 10 minutes) and let cool. Combine all the ingredients in a large bowl and mix with Orange Dressing.

Orange Dressing
¾ cup orange juice
2 tablespoons olive oil
1 tablespoon balsamic vinegar

½ teaspoon salt
⅛ teaspoon pepper

Mix together all ingredients and add to salad.

COCONUT RICE SALAD

½ cup brown rice
1 cup orange juice
2 tablespoons sucanat or brown sugar
⅛ teaspoon salt
1 teaspoon cinnamon
1 cup coconut milk
1 can mandarin oranges
1 cup shredded or flaked coconut, toasted

Soak rice in 2 cups water for 4 hours or overnight. Drain and add orange juice, sugar, and salt. Cook rice in orange juice for 60 minutes or until juice is absorbed and rice is tender. Remove from heat, stir in cinnamon, and chill. Mix coconut milk and mandarin oranges into the rice. Salad will be somewhat runny and will need to be served in bowls. Just before serving top generously with toasted coconut.

CHAPTER 4

Sauces, Gravies, and Flavored Oils

SAUCES

TARTAR SAUCE

1 cup Coconut Mayonnaise (page 41)
3 scallions, minced
1 tablespoon parsley, minced
1 tablespoon fresh tarragon, minced
¼ cup dill pickle relish
2 tablespoons capers
1 teaspoon prepared Dijon-style mustard
½ teaspoon sugar
2 tablespoons red wine vinegar

Mix all ingredients, cover, and chill. Serve with seafood.

QUICK TARTAR SAUCE

1 cup Coconut Mayonnaise (page 41)
¼ cup dill pickle relish
3 scallions, minced

Mix all ingredients, cover, and chill.

GUACAMOLE

1 avocado
2 scallions, diced
½ teaspoon lemon juice
⅛ teaspoon salt
¼ teaspoon onion powder
⅛ teaspoon chili powder
2 tablespoons Coconut Mayonnaise (page 41)

Pit and mash avocado with fork. Stir in scallions, lemon juice, salt, onion powder, and chili powder. Blend in mayonnaise. Serve as a dip or spread.

FRUIT SAUCE ♥

This is a great sauce to use as a flavoring for hot cereal, a spread on toast, a filling for crepes, or a topping on pancakes, waffles, and French toast.

1 tablespoon cornstarch
1 cup coconut milk
⅓ cup honey
Dash of salt
1 cup fruit*
1 teaspoon lemon juice
¼ teaspoon vanilla
⅛ teaspoon almond extract

In a saucepan mix cornstarch into coconut milk until dissolved. Add honey and salt. Bring to a boil, reduce heat and simmer, stirring constantly until thickened. Add fruit and continue to simmer 5 minutes. Remove from heat and add lemon juice, vanilla, and almond extract. Taste for sweetness and add more honey if desired.

*Use fresh or canned cherries, peaches, apricots, apples, strawberries, raspberries, boysenberries, or blueberries. If using peaches or apples, add ½ teaspoon cinnamon and a dash of nutmeg.

Reduced Sugar Fruit Sauce

Make Fruit Sauce as directed but omit the honey and add ⅛ teaspoon of powdered stevia or more for desired sweetness.

COCONUT SAUCE ♥

This is a rich tasting coconut flavored sauce that goes well over pancakes, fresh fruit, rice, or desserts.

1 can (14 ounces) coconut milk
½ cup sugar
¼ cup cornstarch
½ teaspoon imitation coconut extract (optional)

Mix together coconut milk, sugar, and cornstarch in a medium saucepan. Bring mixture to a boil, reduce heat, and simmer for about 5 minutes, stirring constantly. Mixture will thicken. Add coconut extract. Remove from heat and cool. Serve lukewarm. Can be stored in an airtight container in the refrigerator for about a week.

Reduced Sugar Coconut Sauce
Make Coconut Sauce according to directions but reduce sugar to ¼ cup and add a dash or two of powdered stevia.

COCONUT CUSTARD SAUCE ♥

1 can (14 ounces) coconut milk
½ cup grated coconut
5 tablespoons sugar
Dash of salt
4 egg yolks, lightly beaten
½ teaspoon vanilla
¼ teaspoon almond extract

Put milk, coconut, sugar, and salt in a saucepan. Bring to a boil, reduce heat, and simmer for 5 minutes, stirring constantly. Remove from heat and slowly stir about half of the hot mixture into egg yolks. Combine with the rest of the hot mixture, stir, and heat 2 to 3 minutes until thickened. Remove from heat and add vanilla and almond extract. May be served hot or cold. Can be eaten as is or served over cake, pancakes, or fresh fruit.

Reduced Sugar Coconut Custard Sauce
Prepare as directed but reduce sugar to 2-3 tablespoons and add up to ⅛ teaspoon of powdered stevia.

CHEESE SAUCES ♥
Cheese sauces make great toppings or dips for a variety of raw vegetables as well as French fries, corn chips, and crackers. They also make great toppings for cooked vegetables, pasta, baked potatoes, eggs, casseroles, and other dishes.

Creamy Cheese Sauce

This is the basic cheese sauce recipe. Variations are described below.

3 tablespoons butter
2 teaspoons cornstarch
¼ teaspoon salt
1 cup coconut milk
1 cup shredded sharp cheddar cheese (6 ounces)

Melt butter in saucepan over low heat. Mix cornstarch and salt in coconut milk and add to saucepan. Stir constantly until mixture thickens and bubbles. Remove from heat and add cheese, stirring until melted. Makes about 1½ cups. For thinner sauce, add a little more coconut milk.

Thick Cheddar Cheese Sauce

Follow the directions for the cheese sauce above but increase cornstarch to 4 teaspoons and cheddar cheese to 1¼ cups. This sauce is very thick and makes a good replacement for soft cheese in recipes.

Tex-Mex Cheddar Cheese Sauce

Make the Thick Cheddar Cheese Sauce as directed and add ½ cup salsa.

Garlic Cheese Sauce

Make the Creamy Cheese Sauce as directed but sauté 6 cloves of diced garlic with the butter. Use more garlic if you prefer a stronger flavor.

Crab Cheese Sauce

Make the Creamy Cheese Sauce as directed but delete the salt and add two 7½ ounce cans of crabmeat as mixture begins to boil. Cook for 1 minute longer, remove from heat, and add cheese and 1 teaspoon of fish sauce.*

Shrimp Cheese Sauce

Make the Creamy Cheese Sauce as directed but delete the salt and add 1½ cups baby shrimp as mixture begins to boil. Cook for 1 minute longer, remove from heat, and add cheese and 1 teaspoon of fish sauce.*

*Fish sauce is available in the Asian section of the grocery store.

Mushroom and Onion Cheese Sauce

Sauté 1 cup of chopped mushroom and ½ cup diced onions in butter, olive oil, or coconut oil until tender. Make the Creamy Cheese Sauce as directed and add to the mushroom and onions.

GRAVIES

Mashed potatoes and gravy are a traditional favorite combination. Gravy, however, isn't just for mashed potatoes. The gravies described below taste great combined with a variety of foods. Try them on pasta, biscuits, toast, steamed vegetables, and rice.

VEGETARIAN GRAVY

½ cup coconut oil
⅓ cup onion, chopped
5 cloves garlic, minced
½ cup flour
2 cups vegetable broth
3 tablespoons soy sauce
½ teaspoon dried sage
½ teaspoon salt
¼ teaspoon pepper

Heat oil in saucepan over medium heat. Sauté onion and garlic until soft, about 5 minutes. Stir in flour and cook 4 minutes. Add vegetable broth, soy sauce, sage, salt, and pepper. Bring to a boil, reduce heat, and simmer until thickened, stirring constantly.

WHITE CREAM GRAVY

3 tablespoons butter
⅓ cup onion, chopped
5 cloves garlic, minced
3 tablespoons flour
1 can (14 ounces) coconut milk
½ teaspoon salt
¼ teaspoon pepper

Heat butter in saucepan over medium heat. Sauté onion and garlic until soft, about 5 minutes. Stir in flour and cook 4 minutes. Add coconut milk, salt, and pepper. Bring to a boil, reduce heat, and simmer until thickened, stirring constantly.

CHICKEN GRAVY ❤

3 tablespoons butter
⅓ cup onion, chopped
5 cloves garlic, minced
1 ½ tablespoons cornstarch
1 cup coconut milk
1 cup chicken broth
1 teaspoon dried sage
½ teaspoon salt
¼ teaspoon pepper

Heat butter in saucepan over medium heat. Sauté onion and garlic until soft and lightly browned, about 8 minutes. Mix cornstarch into coconut milk until thoroughly dissolved. Add coconut milk, broth, sage, salt, and pepper to hot mixture. Bring to a boil, reduce heat, and simmer until thickened, stirring constantly.

CURRY GRAVY

3 tablespoons butter
⅓ cup onion, chopped
5 cloves garlic, minced
1 ½ tablespoons cornstarch
1 cup coconut milk
1 cup chicken broth
1 teaspoon curry powder or garam masala
½ teaspoon salt
¼ teaspoon pepper

Heat butter in saucepan over medium heat. Sauté onion and garlic until soft and lightly browned, about 8 minutes. Mix cornstarch into coconut milk until thoroughly dissolved. Add coconut milk, broth, curry powder or garam masala, salt, and pepper to hot mixture. Bring to a boil, reduce heat, and simmer until thickened, stirring constantly.

SAUSAGE GRAVY

1 pound sausage
⅓ cup onion, chopped
5 cloves garlic, minced
2 tablespoons cornstarch
1 can (14 ounces) coconut milk
½ cup water
1 teaspoon dried sage
½ teaspoon paprika
½ teaspoon salt
¼ teaspoon pepper

In a skillet cook sausage, onion, and garlic until meat is browned and vegetables are tender. Mix cornstarch into water until thoroughly dissolved. Mix water, coconut milk, sage, paprika, salt, and pepper into hot mixture. Bring to a boil, reduce heat, and simmer until thickened, stirring constantly.

Spicy Sausage Gravy
Make Sausage Gravy as directed but omit the sage and add ¼ cup of salsa. Add a dash or two of cayenne pepper if desired.

CHUNKY CHICKEN GRAVY ♥

3 tablespoons butter
½ cup onion, chopped
5 cloves garlic, minced
2 tablespoons cornstarch
1 cup chicken broth or water
1 cup chicken, cut into small bite-size pieces
1 can (4 ounces) mushrooms
1 can (14 ounces) coconut milk
1 teaspoon dried sage
½ teaspoon salt
¼ teaspoon pepper

Heat butter in saucepan over medium heat. Sauté onion and garlic until soft and lightly browned, about 8 minutes. Mix cornstarch into broth or water until thoroughly dissolved. Add water and remaining ingredients to hot mixture. Bring to a boil, reduce heat, and simmer until thickened, stirring constantly.

FLAVORED OILS

Coconut oil generally has a mild flavor. Some brands are completely flavorless. The mild flavor makes the oil ideal for general cooking purposes, but is often too bland as a spread or topping. A variety of flavors can be added to the oil to enhance its taste and aroma. Flavored oils can be used as a spread in place of butter, used as a dip for bread and chips, or as a topping on meats, steamed or raw vegetables, potatoes, rice, pasta, and popcorn. They also make excellent salad dressings or can be used as the base for salad dressings. Because additional heat can change their character, these oils are used for flavoring, not for cooking.

There are two basic methods for flavoring oils. Flavoring ingredients such as nuts and shrimp that taste best when cooked or roasted are heated with the oil. These are called *heated oils*. Ingredients that taste better raw or lightly cooked, like herbs, are covered with hot oil and left to sit for 30 minutes. These are called *infused oils*. Store oils in the refrigerator and use within a couple of days.

HEATED OILS
When you use the heating method to flavor oil, the saucepan should be placed on low heat. Cook ingredients just enough to extract the flavor, then remove from heat, put into a separate container, and let cool. Oil retains heat for some time and will continue to cook even after it has been taken off the burner. Remove from heat before the ingredients have been completely cooked and allow the hot oil to finish the cooking. Do not overcook. You may strain the flavoring ingredients and separate them from the oil before using, or eat them along with the oil. If they are not overcooked, they usually add to the flavor and enjoyment of the oil. When making these oils, use an equal amount of coconut oil and flavoring ingredient. For example, if you have ¼ cup flavoring ingredient, cook it in ¼ cup oil. The flavored oils below use the heating method.

Toasted Coconut Oil

Toasting dried coconut in coconut oil gives the oil a wonderful flavor. This oil makes an excellent spread in place of butter. Sauté until coconut is lightly browned. Remove from heat and cool. You can use any type of dried coconut: grated, shredded, or flaked. Keep the coconut in the oil when you use it.

Sesame Seed Oil

This oil makes a great tasting topping on vegetables and salad dressing. Sauté sesame seeds until lightly browned. Do not overcook. Keep in mind that oil remains hot even after the pan is removed from the heat, so the sesame seeds will continue to cook for a few minutes. Keep the seeds in the oil when used.

Almond Oil

If you like almonds, you'll love this oil. Crush or finely chop almonds and toast them until lightly browned. Keep the almonds in the oil when used.

Garlic Oil

This lightly flavored oil will give foods just enough garlic flavor to awaken your taste buds. Dice garlic and sauté it in oil until lightly browned. Remove the garlic and use just the oil.

Onion Oil

This oil will give food a hint of onion flavor. Try on popcorn or bread. Tastes great with vegetables. Chop onion and sauté until tender and lightly browned. Use the oil with or without the onion bits.

Shrimp Oil

Dice shrimp and cook in hot oil for only a couple of minutes. Shrimp cooks quickly, avoid overcooking. Keep the shrimp in the oil when used. Makes an excellent salad dressing or topping on vegetables. You can spruce it up by adding a little lemon juice, salt, and pepper.

INFUSED OILS

With the infusion method, oil is heated in a saucepan until hot. *Remove pan from heat,* add flavoring ingredients, pour into a separate container, and let sit for about 30 minutes to allow the flavor to infuse or migrate into the oil. Always add flavoring ingredients to pan *before* pouring into separate container to avoid splattering hot oil. Strain or remove flavoring ingredients before using the oil. When making these oils, use equal amounts of coconut oil and flavoring ingredient unless otherwise directed. So if you have ¼ cup flavoring ingredient, mix in ¼ cup oil. The flavored oils below use the infusion method.

Lemon Oil

Lemon gives many foods a welcome boost in flavor. This oil has a mild lemon flavor that will add just enough flavor to perk up your taste buds. Use finely chopped lemon peel, not the fruit. Serve with fish, asparagus, artichokes, or broccoli.

Orange Oil

Like lemon, the flavor of orange can add dimension to foods. Use finely chopped or grated orange peal.

Ginger Oil

Ginger is a wonderful spice that can be used in main dishes, desserts, and beverages. Use finely diced fresh ginger. Remove ginger before using.

Red Pepper Oil

If you want to add some spice to a dish, this oil can do the job. But watch out, this oil is hot! A little can go a long way. Infuse oil with crushed red pepper. You can use the oil with or without the red pepper pieces.

Herb Oil

You can give oil most any type of herb flavor. Fresh, diced herbs work best but dried herbs can also be used. Types of herbs you can use include dill, bay leaves, sage, lemon grass, coriander, and others.

Italian Herb Oil

This nice all-purpose herbal blend uses several different herbs. Use this oil as a dip for chips and raw vegetables, a topping on steamed vegetables, a spread on bread, a salad dressing, or as a topping for popcorn.

3 ½ tablespoons coconut oil
2 tablespoons of onion, finely diced
1 tablespoon garlic, finely diced or crushed
½ teaspoon basil
½ teaspoon oregano
¼ teaspoon paprika

¼ teaspoon salt
⅛ teaspoon black pepper (or cayenne pepper)

Heat oil until hot and remove from heat. Combine all remaining ingredients in a small container and add to hot oil. Pour the hot oil into a separate container and let sit for 30 minutes. Do not strain oil before using.

CHAPTER 5

Soups and Chowders

CHICKEN AND DUMPLINGS ♥

4 cups chicken broth
½ cup chopped onion
½ cup chopped celery
½ cup sliced carrot
½ cup flour
1 can (14 ounces) coconut milk or cream
½ cup peas
2 cups cut-up chicken
1 teaspoon salt
¼ teaspoon pepper
½ teaspoon thyme
Dumplings (see below)

Bring chicken broth to a boil in a 3-quart saucepan. Add onion, celery, and carrot; reduce heat and simmer for 30 minutes. Mix flour into coconut milk; stir into hot broth. Bring to a boil and add peas, chicken, salt, pepper, and thyme; reduce heat to a simmer. Drop dumplings into soup, cover, and simmer for 20 minutes. Serves 6.

Dumplings
1 cup flour
½ teaspoon salt
1½ teaspoons baking powder
½ cup coconut milk
1 egg

Mix flour, salt, and baking powder together. In a separate bowl mix coconut milk and egg together. Combine the wet and dry ingredients. Form the dough into 1¼-inch balls. Coat each one in flour and drop into soup. Cook covered for 20 minutes. Makes 12 dumplings.

HEARTY CHICKEN STEW ♥

4 cups chicken broth
½ large onion, chopped
1 stalk celery, chopped
1 cup green beans

3 medium red potatoes, chopped
¼ cup flour
1 can (14 ounces) coconut milk or cream
½ cup peas
2 cups chicken, cut into bite-size pieces
1 teaspoons salt
⅛ teaspoon pepper
½ teaspoon ground sage

Bring chicken broth to a boil in a 3-quart saucepan. Add onion, celery, green beans, and potatoes; reduce heat and simmer for 20 minutes. Mix flour into coconut milk; stir into hot broth. Bring to a boil and add peas, chicken, salt, pepper, and sage; reduce heat to a simmer and cook for 10 minutes.

CREAM OF ASPARAGUS SOUP

1 pound asparagus, washed, trimmed, and cut in 1-inch pieces
½ cup chopped celery
¼ cup chopped onion
1 cup water
2 tablespoons extra virgin olive oil
2 tablespoons flour
1 can (14 ounces) coconut milk
1¼ teaspoon salt
⅛ teaspoon pepper
¼ teaspoon tarragon

Simmer asparagus, celery, and onion in water for 20 minutes or until very tender. Puree, a little at a time, in an electric blender at low speed. Heat olive oil in saucepan over medium heat; blend in flour and cook until lightly browned, stirring frequently. Add coconut milk slowly, stirring until smooth. Mix in puree, salt, pepper, and tarragon, stirring occasionally, until hot but not boiling.

CREAM OF BROCCOLI SOUP

2 cups chopped broccoli
½ cup chopped celery
¼ cup chopped onion

1 cup water
2 tablespoons butter or coconut oil
2 tablespoons flour
1 can (14 ounces) coconut milk
1 ¼ teaspoon salt
⅛ teaspoon pepper
¼ teaspoon basil

Simmer broccoli, celery, and onion in water for 20 minutes or until very tender. Puree, a little at a time, in an electric blender at low speed. Heat butter in saucepan over medium heat; blend in flour and cook until lightly browned, stirring frequently. Add coconut milk slowly, stirring until smooth. Mix in puree, salt, pepper, and basil, stirring occasionally, until hot but not boiling.

CREAM OF CAULIFLOWER SOUP

2 cups chopped cauliflower
½ cup chopped celery
¼ cup chopped onion
1 cup water
2 tablespoons butter or coconut oil
2 tablespoons flour
1 can (14 ounces) coconut milk
1 ¼ teaspoon salt
⅛ teaspoon white pepper
¼ teaspoon curry powder

Simmer cauliflower, celery, and onion in water for 20 minutes or until very tender. Puree, a little at a time, in an electric blender at low speed. Heat butter in saucepan over medium heat; blend in flour and cook until lightly browned, stirring frequently. Add coconut milk slowly, stirring until smooth. Mix in puree, salt, pepper, and curry powder, stirring occasionally, until hot but not boiling.

CURRIED CREAM OF CAULIFLOWER SOUP

½ cup onion, chopped
½ tablespoon curry powder

⅛ teaspoon saffron
2 tablespoons coconut oil
½ cup apple, shopped
3 cups cauliflower, chopped
2 cups water or chicken broth
1 teaspoon salt
⅛ teaspoon white pepper
½ cup coconut milk

Sauté onions, curry, and saffron in coconut oil for 2 minutes, stirring often. Add apple and cook another 5 minutes. Add cauliflower, water, salt, and pepper. Bring to boil, reduce heat and simmer for 15 minutes until cauliflower is tender. Add coconut milk and simmer 2 minutes. Puree soup in blender until smooth. Serve hot.

CREAM OF ARTICHOKE SOUP

½ cup chopped celery
¼ cup chopped onion
2 cloves garlic
2 tablespoons coconut oil or butter
2 tablespoons flour
1 cup water
1 can (14 ounces) coconut milk
1 can (14 ounces) artichoke hearts, drained and rinsed
1 teaspoon salt
¼ teaspoon white pepper
¼ teaspoon thyme

Sauté celery, onion, and garlic in coconut oil in a heavy saucepan over low heat until vegetables are tender. Stir in flour and cook for 2 minutes. Add water and coconut milk, bring to a boil, reduce heat and simmer for 8 to 10 minutes. Puree half the mixture and all of the artichokes in an electric blender; add to pan. Add remaining ingredients and heat, stirring, 2 to 3 minutes. Makes 4 servings.

CREAM OF SPINACH SOUP

1 pound fresh spinach, washed, and chopped*
1 stalk celery, chopped
½ medium onion, chopped
3 cloves garlic, chopped
2 cups water
1¼ teaspoons salt
¾ teaspoon lemon pepper
1 can (14 ounces) coconut milk

In a large saucepan simmer spinach, celery, onion, garlic, salt, and lemon pepper in water for 30 minutes or until very tender. Add coconut milk and puree in an electric blender at low speed. Serve hot.

*You may use a 10-ounce package of frozen spinach if desired.

CREAM OF POTATO SOUP

1 pound potatoes, peeled and cut in 1-inch chunks
½ cup chopped celery
¼ cup chopped onion
1 cup water
2 tablespoons extra virgin olive oil
2 tablespoons flour
1 can (14 ounces) coconut milk
1¼ teaspoon salt
⅛ teaspoon white pepper
¼ teaspoon dill

Simmer potatoes, celery, and onion in water for 20 minutes or until very tender. Puree, a little at a time, in an electric blender at low speed. Heat olive oil in saucepan over medium heat; blend in flour and cook until lightly browned, stirring frequently. Add coconut milk slowly, stirring until smooth. Mix in puree, salt, pepper, and dill, stirring occasionally, until hot but not boiling.

CREAM OF MUSHROOM SOUP

8 ounces chopped mushrooms
¼ cup chopped onion
2 tablespoons butter
2 tablespoons cornstarch
1 cup water
1 can (14 ounces) coconut milk
1 teaspoon salt
⅛ teaspoon white pepper
1 teaspoon Worcestershire sauce

Sauté mushrooms and onion in butter in a heavy saucepan over low heat 5 to 7 minutes. Blend cornstarch and water together and add to saucepan; heat, stirring, 3 to 4 minutes. Add coconut milk, cover, and simmer over lowest heat 12 to 15 minutes, stirring occasionally. Puree half the mixture in an electric blender; return to pan. Add remaining ingredients and heat, stirring, 2 to 3 minutes. Makes 4 servings.

CREAMY ZUCCHINI SOUP

½ cup onion, chopped
2 garlic cloves, minced
2 tablespoons coconut oil
3 cups water or chicken broth
1 potato (about 1 cup), chopped
1 large carrot, sliced
4 medium zucchini, cut in 1-inch pieces
1 cup coconut milk
1 tablespoon fresh basil or 1 teaspoon dried
1 teaspoon salt
⅛ teaspoon white pepper

Sauté onion and garlic in coconut oil for 2 minutes. Add water, potato, carrot, and zucchini; bring to a boil, reduce heat, and simmer 15 minutes until vegetables are tender. Add coconut milk, basil, salt, and pepper and simmer 5 minutes. Puree in blender until smooth. Serve hot.

CREAMY TOMATO SOUP

2 tablespoons yellow onion, minced
2 tablespoons extra virgin olive oil
2 tablespoons flour
½ cup water
¾ cup tomato sauce
1 can (14 ounces) coconut milk
½ teaspoon basil
½ teaspoon oregano
1 teaspoons salt
⅛ teaspoon pepper
½ teaspoon garlic powder

Sauté onion in olive oil in a heavy saucepan for about 4 minutes until limp, blend in flour. Add water, tomato sauce, coconut milk, herbs, salt, pepper, and garlic powder and bring to a boil. Reduce heat and simmer for 10 minutes, stirring occasionally. Serve hot.

CREAMY TOMATO VEGETABLE SOUP

¼ cup yellow onion, minced
½ cup celery, chopped
½ cup carrot, chopped
2 tablespoons extra virgin olive oil
2 tablespoons flour
½ cup water
½ cup peas
¾ cup tomato sauce
1 can (14 ounces) coconut milk
½ teaspoon basil
½ teaspoon oregano
1 teaspoons salt
⅛ teaspoon pepper
½ teaspoon garlic powder

Sauté onion, celery, and carrot in olive oil in a heavy saucepan for about 4 minutes until limp, blend in flour. Add water, peas, tomato sauce, coconut milk, herbs, salt, pepper, and garlic powder and bring to a boil. Reduce heat and simmer for 10 minutes, stirring occasionally. Serve hot.

TOMATO SHRIMP SOUP

2 tablespoons yellow onion, minced
2 tablespoons extra virgin olive oil
2 tablespoons flour
½ cup water
¾ cup tomato sauce
1 can (14 ounces) coconut milk
½ teaspoon basil
½ teaspoon oregano
1 teaspoons salt
⅛ teaspoon pepper
½ teaspoon garlic powder
½ cup baby shrimp

Sauté onion in olive oil in a heavy saucepan for about 4 minutes until limp, blend in flour. Add water, tomato sauce, coconut milk, herbs, salt, pepper, garlic powder, and shrimp and bring to a boil. Reduce heat and simmer for 10 minutes, stirring occasionally. Serve hot.

NEW ENGLAND CLAM CHOWDER

1½ cups water
½ cup yellow onion, peeled and minced
1 stalk celery, chopped
2 cups red potatoes, diced
1 teaspoon salt
⅛ teaspoon white pepper
1 can (14 ounces) coconut milk or cream
1 can (6½ or 8 ounces) minced or chopped clams

In a medium saucepan, heat water, onion, celery, potatoes, salt, and pepper to boiling. Reduce heat and simmer for about 20 minutes or until potatoes are tender. Add coconut milk and clams, including the clam juice. Cook for about 5 minutes until heated through.

DELUXE CLAM CHOWDER ❤

½ cup water ½ cup yellow onion, peeled and minced
4 cloves garlic, minced
1 stalk celery, chopped
2 cups red potatoes, diced
1 teaspoon salt
⅛ teaspoon white pepper
1 can (14 ounces) coconut milk or cream
1 can (8 ounce) minced or chopped clams
1 bottle (8 ounces) clam juice
1 tablespoon butter (optional)
¼ teaspoon paprika

In a medium saucepan, heat water, onion, garlic, celery, potatoes, salt, and pepper to boiling. Reduce heat and simmer for about 20 minutes or until potatoes are tender. Add coconut milk and clams, including the clam juice, and butter. Cook for about 5 minutes until heated through. Sprinkle top with paprika and serve.

FISH CHOWDER

1 pound fresh or frozen fish fillets
1 ½ cups water
½ cup yellow onion, peeled and minced
2 cups red potatoes, diced
1 teaspoon salt
⅛ teaspoon white pepper
1 can (14 ounces) coconut milk or cream

Cut fish in bite size pieces. In a medium saucepan, heat water, fish, onion, potatoes, salt, and pepper to boiling. Reduce heat and simmer for about 20 minutes or until potatoes are tender. Add coconut milk and cook for about 5 minutes until heated through.

SHRIMP CHOWDER

3 strips bacon
½ cup yellow onion, peeled and minced
1 ½ cups water
2 cups red potatoes, diced
1 teaspoon salt
⅛ teaspoon white pepper
1 can (14 ounces) coconut milk or cream
2 teaspoons fish sauce*
½ pound fresh or frozen baby shrimp

Cook bacon until crisp, remove and set aside. Sauté onion in bacon drippings until tender. In a medium saucepan heat water, potatoes, salt, and pepper to boiling. Reduce heat and simmer for about 15 minutes or until potatoes are tender. Add cooked onions, coconut milk, fish sauce, and shrimp. Cook for about 5 minutes until heated through. Serve with bacon crumbled on top.

*Fish sauce is available in the Asian section of the grocery store.

CRAB CHOWDER

1 medium onion, chopped
2 stalks celery, chopped
2 cloves garlic, chopped
2 tablespoons butter or coconut oil
4 cups chicken broth
4 red potatoes, chopped
1 can (14¾ ounces) cream-style corn
½ teaspoon salt
½ teaspoon black pepper
¼ cup flour
1 can (14 ounces) coconut milk
8 ounces crabmeat
2 tablespoons fish sauce*
1 teaspoon thyme

In a large saucepan, sauté onion, celery, and garlic in butter until tender. Add chicken broth, potatoes, corn, salt, and pepper. Bring to a boil, reduce heat, and simmer 20 minutes or until potatoes are tender. Mix flour into coconut milk and add to chowder along with crabmeat, fish sauce, and thyme. Cook, stirring frequently, for another 5 to 6 minutes, until chowder is slightly thickened.

*Fish sauce is available in the Asian section of the grocery store.

CORN CHOWDER

½ cup onion, chopped
½ cup bell pepper, chopped
2 tablespoons coconut oil or bacon drippings
2 tablespoons flour
¾ cup water
1 can (14 ounces) coconut milk
2 cups frozen or canned corn
1 teaspoon salt
¼ teaspoon pepper
1 jar (4 ounces) pimento
2 teaspoons fish sauce*
4 slices bacon, crisp-cooked and crumbled (optional)

Sauté onion and bell pepper in coconut oil or bacon drippings in large saucepan until tender. Add flour and cook for 3 to 4 minutes. Add water, coconut milk, corn, salt, and pepper. Bring to a boil stirring constantly; reduce heat, and simmer for about 10 minutes. Puree half the mixture in an electric blender; return to pan. Add pimento and fish sauce heat, stirring, 2 to 3 minutes. Serve topped with crumbled bacon.

*Fish sauce is available in the Asian section of the grocery store.

CORN AND POTATO CHOWDER

2 medium diced, pared potatoes
1 medium onion, thinly sliced and separated into rings
½ cup chopped celery
1 teaspoon salt
½ cup water
2 cups whole kernel corn

1 can (4 ounces) pimento
1 can (14 ounces) coconut milk or cream
¼ teaspoon dried marjoram, crushed
⅛ teaspoon white pepper
1 tablespoon butter (optional)
5 slices bacon, crisp-cooked and crumbled (optional)

In saucepan, combine potatoes, onion, celery, salt, and water. Cover; cook 15 minutes or until tender. Stir in corn, pimento, coconut milk, marjoram, and pepper; simmer for 5 minutes. Add butter if you like and serve topped with crumbled bacon.

OYSTER STEW ♥

1 ½ cups water
½ cup yellow onion, peeled and minced
1 stalk celery, chopped
2 cups potatoes, diced
1 teaspoon salt
⅛ teaspoon white pepper
1 can (14 ounces) coconut milk or cream
1 tablespoon butter
1 can (8 ounces) oysters

In a medium saucepan heat water, onion, celery, potatoes, salt, and pepper to boiling. Reduce heat and simmer for about 20 minutes or until potatoes are tender. Add coconut milk, butter, and oysters, including the oyster juice. Cook for about 5 minutes until heated through.

POTATO SOUP

1 small yellow onion, peeled and minced
½ cup chopped celery
2 tablespoons coconut oil
½ cup chopped mushrooms
2 cups diced, peeled potatoes
2 cups water or chicken broth
1 teaspoon salt
1 can (14 ounces) coconut milk or cream
⅛ teaspoon white pepper
1 tablespoon minced parsley, chives, or dill

Sauté onion and celery in coconut oil in a heavy saucepan over moderate heat 5 minutes until limp; add mushrooms, potatoes, water, and salt, cover and simmer 10 to 15 minutes until potatoes are nearly tender. Add coconut milk and pepper and simmer uncovered, stirring occasionally, 3 to 5 minutes until potatoes are tender. Sprinkle with parsley, chives, or dill and serve. Crumbled bacon also goes well as a garnish.

POTATO AND SAUSAGE SOUP

1 pound sausage
¼ cup onion, chopped
½ cup chopped green pepper
3 tablespoons flour
3 cups water
1 can (14 ounces) coconut milk
3 red potatoes, chopped
1 teaspoon salt
⅛ teaspoon pepper
1 teaspoon ground sage

Cook sausage, onion, and green pepper in heavy saucepan until meat is browned and vegetables are tender. Stir in flour, cook for 1 minute. Add water, coconut milk, potatoes, salt, and pepper and bring to a boil; reduce heat and simmer about 20 minutes or until potatoes are tender. Add sage and simmer 5 minutes.

HAM AND POTATO SOUP

1 meaty ham bone (1 ½ pounds)
½ medium onion, chopped
1 stalk celery, chopped
1 carrot, chopped
3 red potatoes, chopped
1 can (14 ounces) coconut milk
1 teaspoon salt
⅛ teaspoon pepper
¼ teaspoon marjoram

Combine 4 cups water, ham bone, onion, celery, and carrot in heavy saucepan. Bring to a boil; cover, reduce heat, and simmer 2 hours. Remove bone; cut off meat and dice. Return meat to soup; add potatoes, coconut milk, salt, pepper, and marjoram. Simmer about 20 minutes or until potatoes are tender.

CHICKEN AND RICE STEW

3 tablespoons coconut oil
1 small yellow onion, peeled and minced
1 medium carrot, peeled and diced fine
1 stalk celery, diced fine
½ green pepper, cored, seeded and minced
¼ cup flour
1 tablespoon curry powder
¼ teaspoon nutmeg
1 teaspoon ground cloves
1 teaspoon dried parsley
3 cups chicken broth
1 teaspoon salt
⅛ teaspoon pepper

1 cup chopped tomatoes
1 cup cooked, diced chicken
1 can (14 ounces) coconut milk
1 cup cooked rice

Heat coconut oil in a large saucepan, add onion, carrot, celery, and green pepper and cook 8 to 10 minutes until onion is slightly golden. Stir in flour, curry powder, and nutmeg; add cloves, parsley, broth, salt, pepper, and tomatoes; cover and simmer 30 minutes. Strain broth, separating vegetables from liquid; puree vegetables in an electric blender at low speed. Stir puree into broth, return to heat, add chicken and coconut milk; cook, stirring occasionally, for 5 or 6 minutes. Add cooked rice and continue to cook until heated through.

RED LENTIL SOUP

2 tablespoons coconut oil
1 large onion, chopped (2 cups)
3 medium carrots, peeled and chopped
4 cups water
1 can (14 ounces) coconut milk
1 cup red lentils
3 cloves garlic, chopped
1 bay leaf
2 teaspoons salt
¼ teaspoon ground ginger
1 tablespoon curry powder
½ cup chopped cilantro

Heat coconut oil in a large saucepan over medium heat. Add onions and carrots and cook, stirring frequently, until vegetables start to brown, about 10 minutes. Add 4 cups water, coconut milk, lentils, garlic, bay leaf, salt, ginger, and curry powder. Cover and bring to a boil. Reduce heat and simmer, partially covered, for 35 to 40 minutes or until lentils are tender, stirring occasionally. Add cilantro and cook 3 additional minutes. Remove bay leaf and discard. Puree soup in batches in blender until velvety smooth. Serve hot.

CREAMY CHEESE AND BROCCOLI SOUP

4 cups chicken broth
½ medium onion, chopped
1 stalk celery, chopped
½ head broccoli, chopped
1 teaspoon salt
⅛ teaspoon pepper
½ teaspoon basil
2 cups Creamy Cheese Sauce (page 58)

Bring chicken broth to a boil in a 3-quart saucepan. Add onion, celery, broccoli, salt, pepper, and basil. Reduce heat and simmer for 30 minutes until vegetables are very tender. Puree soup in a blender until smooth. Return to pan and add Creamy Cheese Sauce. At moderately low temperature stir cheese sauce into soup until well blended and hot. Remove from heat and serve.

CHEESE AND POTATO SOUP

1 small yellow onion, peeled and minced
1 stalk celery, chopped
2 tablespoons coconut oil
4 ounces mushrooms, chopped
2 potatoes, chopped
2 cups water
2 cups chicken broth
1 teaspoon salt
¼ teaspoon pepper
1 cup cooked chicken, cut into bite-size pieces
1 teaspoon minced dill
3 cups Creamy Cheese Sauce (page 58)

Sauté onion and celery in coconut oil in a heavy saucepan over moderate heat 5 minutes until limp; add mushrooms, potatoes, water, chicken broth, salt, and pepper, cover and simmer about 15 minutes or until potatoes are tender. Mix in chicken, dill, and Creamy Cheddar Cheese Sauce and simmer for 5 minutes, stirring frequently. Remove from heat and serve.

BEEFY CHEESE SOUP ♥

1 tablespoon coconut oil
1 pound ground beef
1 medium onion, chopped
4 cups water
1 cup salsa
2 potatoes, chopped
1½ cup green beans, chopped
2 cups Creamy Cheese Sauce (page 58)
1½ teaspoon salt
¼ teaspoon pepper
½ teaspoon thyme

Heat oil in large saucepan. Cook ground beef and onion until onion is tender and beef is browned. Add water, salsa, potatoes, and green beans. Bring to a boil, reduce heat, cover, and simmer for 15 minutes or until potatoes are tender. Stir in Creamy Cheese Sauce, salt, pepper, and thyme. Simmer 5 more minutes and serve.

TAMALE SOUP ♥

1 tablespoon coconut oil
1 pound ground beef
1 small onion, chopped
½ bell pepper, chopped
4 cups water
3 tablespoons flour
1 cup Creamy Cheese Sauce (page 58)
1 cup cooked pinto beans
½ cup corn
1 can (8 ounces) tomato sauce
½ cup salsa
1 teaspoon chili powder
1 teaspoon cumin
1 teaspoon salt
Corn Bread Dumplings (below)

Heat coconut oil in large saucepan. Sauté ground beef, onion, and bell pepper until vegetables are tender and meat is browned. Mix water and flour together and pour into saucepan. Add Creamy Cheese Sauce, pinto beans, corn, tomato sauce, salsa, chili powder, cumin and salt; bring to a boil; reduce heat to a simmer for 10 minutes, stirring frequently. Drop Corn Bread Dumplings into hot soup. Cover and simmer for 20 minutes. Serve hot with dumplings.

Corn Bread Dumplings

½ cup coconut milk
1 egg
½ cup cornmeal
¼ cup flour
1 teaspoon baking powder
1 teaspoon sugar
¼ teaspoon salt

Combine coconut milk and egg in a bowl and mix thoroughly. In a separate bowl mix together cornmeal, flour, baking powder, sugar, and salt. Add the dry ingredients to the wet, mixing just until moistened. Form dough into 1-inch balls and roll in flour to coat surface. Drop into hot soup.

BUTTERNUT SOUP

This is a slightly sweet vegetarian soup that even meat eaters would enjoy.

2 tablespoons coconut oil
1 medium onion, chopped
1 carrot, sliced
1 stalk celery, chopped
½ butternut squash, peeled and chopped
1 large tart apple, peeled, cored, and chopped
1 tablespoon ground ginger
2 cups water
1 can (14 ounces) coconut milk
½ teaspoon salt

Heat oil in a large saucepan. Sauté onion, carrot, and celery until tender. Add butternut squash, apple, ginger, water, coconut milk, and salt. Bring to a boil, reduce heat, cover, and simmer for about 40 minutes or until all the vegetables are very soft. Pour into a blender and puree. Serve hot.

THAI CHICKEN AND SHRIMP SOUP

3 cups water or chicken broth
1 cup bottled clam juice
1 tablespoon fish sauce
2 garlic cloves, diced
1 teaspoon ground ginger
½ teaspoon red curry paste
1 (8-ounce) package mushrooms, sliced
2 to 3 chicken breasts, cut into bite-size pieces
4 ounces of snow peas
½ pound shrimp, peeled and deveined
1 can (14 ounces) coconut milk or cream
3 scallions, sliced
2 tablespoons fresh cilantro, chopped

In a large saucepan, combine first 9 ingredients. Bring to a boil, reduce heat, and simmer for 10 minutes. Add shrimp and coconut milk and simmer 5 minutes. Add scallions and cilantro and cook 1 minute. Serve hot.

CHAPTER 6

Main Dishes

CHICKEN STIR-FRY

¼ cup coconut oil
1 medium onion, chopped
3 cloves garlic, chopped
½ bell pepper, chopped
½ head broccoli, sliced
1 pound chicken, cut in bite-size pieces
8 ounces mushroom, sliced
1 can (8½ ounces) bamboo shoots, drained
1 teaspoon ground ginger
1 teaspoon salt
3 tablespoons cornstarch
2½ cups chicken broth or water
¼ cup soy or tamari sauce
Fried wonton skins (below)

Put coconut oil in large skillet. At medium heat, sauté onion, garlic, bell pepper, and broccoli until tender. Add chicken, mushrooms, bamboo shoots, ginger, and salt, cover and cook, stirring occasionally, for about 5 minutes. Mix cornstarch into chicken broth and add to skillet, stirring constantly until thick and bubbly. Remove from heat. Stir in soy or tamari sauce. Serve topped with fried wonton broken into bite-size pieces.

Fried Wonton Skins
Put about ¼-inch of coconut oil in a small skillet. Heat to medium. Put wonton skins in oil one at a time and cook about 30 seconds, turn and cook other side for 1 minute or until golden brown. Remove from oil and place on paper towel to drain. Repeat until you have 6 to 12 cooked wonton skins. Break each wonton skin into several pieces and use as a garnish.

Beef Stir-Fry
Make Chicken Stir-Fry according to instructions but delete chicken and add boneless top loin steak or tenderloin, cut into bite-size pieces.

ALMOND CHICKEN STIR-FRY

¼ cup coconut oil
1 medium onion, chopped

3 cloves garlic, chopped
1 rib celery, chopped
1 bell pepper, chopped
½ cup slivered or chopped almonds
1 pound chicken, cut in bite-size pieces
8 ounces mushrooms, sliced
2 cups mung bean sprouts
2 tablespoons cornstarch
1 cup chicken broth or water
1 teaspoon salt
¼ cup soy or tamari sauce
Fried wonton skins (see above)

Put coconut oil in large skillet. At medium heat, sauté onion, garlic, celery, and bell pepper until tender. Add almonds, chicken, and mushrooms, cover and cook, stirring occasionally, for 4 to 5 minutes. Add bean sprouts and cook 4 to 5 additional minutes. Mix cornstarch into chicken broth and add to skillet, stirring constantly until thick and bubbly. Remove from heat. Stir in salt and soy sauce. Serve topped with fried wontons broken into bite-size pieces.

CHICKEN POT PIE ♥

Pot pies make great meals for lunch or dinner. If you make several at a time, you can refrigerate cooked pies for a quick and easy lunch. Just reheat for a few minutes and serve. They actually taste better the second day. Uncooked pies can be frozen and used at any time for an easy ready-to-cook and eat meal. Frozen pies should be removed from freezer and allowed to thaw for at least 1 hour before baking. You can also thaw frozen pies by putting them in the refrigerator overnight.

2 cups water
1 can (14 ounces) coconut milk
½ cup onion, chopped
½ cup celery, chopped
½ cup peas
1 cup potatoes, chopped
1 teaspoon thyme
1 teaspoon salt
¼ teaspoon pepper
2 cups cut-up cooked chicken

3 tablespoons cornstarch
4 to 5 Tart Pastry Shells (page 174)

Heat water and coconut milk in a large saucepan to boiling. Add vegetables and seasonings. Reduce heat and simmer for 15 minutes. Add meat. Mix cornstarch with ¾ cup water and add to hot mixture stirring constantly until thick and bubbly, remove from heat. Fill *unbaked* pastry shells with hot mixture. Add top crust to pastry shell. Cut a few slits on top of crust. Cook in oven at 400 degrees F for 30 to 35 minutes.

VEGETABLE BEEF POT PIE ♥
This is a good way to use leftover beef. You may also use fresh beef or hamburger if you like.

4 cups water
2 cups beef, chopped
½ cup onion, chopped
1 medium carrot, sliced
½ cup peas
1 potato, chopped
1 teaspoon salt
⅛ teaspoon pepper
1 teaspoon marjoram
½ teaspoon paprika
3 tablespoons cornstarch
4 to 5 Tart Pastry Shells (page 174)

Heat 4 cups of water in a large saucepan to a boil. Add meat, vegetables, and seasonings. Reduce heat and simmer for 15 minutes. Mix cornstarch with ¾ cup cold water and stir. Slowly add to hot mixture, stirring constantly until thick and bubbly; remove from heat. Fill *unbaked* pastry shells with hot mixture. Add top crust to pastry shell. Cut a few slits on top of crust. Cook in oven at 400 degrees F for 30 to 35 minutes.

CREAMY SHRIMP LINGUINE ♥
Linguine is pasta that is long, narrow, and flat. You can substitute spaghetti or any other pasta of your choice in this recipe.

8 ounces linguine
1 medium onion, chopped
4 cloves garlic, chopped
3 tablespoons coconut oil
1 cup mushrooms (about 4 ounces), sliced
½ pound shrimp, peeled, deveined, and tails removed
1 ½ cups Creamy Cheese Sauce (page 58)
2 teaspoons fish sauce*

Prepare pasta according to package directions. To make the sauce: sauté onions and garlic in coconut oil until tender. Add mushrooms and shrimp and cook until shrimp are pink. Stir in Creamy Cheese Sauce and simmer at lowest setting for 2 to 3 minutes. Stir in fish sauce and remove from heat. Serve sauce over hot pasta. Garnish with fresh parsley.

*Fish sauce is available in the Asian section of the grocery store. You may substitute tamari sauce for fish sauce if you desire.

Chicken Linguine
Make the recipe above but replace the shrimp with ½ pound of chicken cut into bite-size pieces, delete fish sauce and add 1 teaspoon salt, ¼ teaspoon pepper, and ½ teaspoon basil.

LASAGNE

1 pound ground beef
1 onion, chopped
6 cloves garlic, diced
2 cans (8 ounces each) tomato sauce
1 can (6 ounces) black olives
½ tablespoon basil
½ tablespoon oregano
1 ½ teaspoon salt
⅛ teaspoon pepper
1 package (8 or 10 ounces) lasagna noodles
2 cups Thick Cheddar Cheese Sauce (page 58)
2 cups mozzarella cheese, shredded

Brown meat, onions, and garlic in skillet until vegetables are tender. Add tomato sauce, olives, basil, oregano, salt, and pepper. Simmer on low heat for 5 minutes. Cook noodles in boiling salted water until tender; drain and rinse. Coat the bottom of a 13x9x2-inch baking dish with Aloha Nu Non-Stick Cooking Oil (page 8) or extra virgin olive oil. Layer one-third of the noodles on the bottom of the baking dish; add meat mixture on top of noodles. Layer another one-third of the noodles on top of the meat mixture; spread Thick Cheddar Cheese Sauce on top of noodles. Layer the remaining one-third of the noodles over the cheddar cheese followed by the mozzarella cheese. Top with croutons (recipe below). Bake at 375 degrees F for 35 minutes. Let stand 10 minutes before serving.

Croutons

Lightly toast 4 slices of bread in toaster. Spread with butter and sprinkle with garlic powder. Cut into small cubes.

CHICKEN AMANDINE

6 ounces noodles
2 tablespoons coconut oil
½ half onion, chopped

3 chicken breasts, cut into bite-size pieces
1/2 cup slivered almonds, lightly toasted
1/2 teaspoon salt
1 cup Creamy Cheese Sauce (page 58)

Make noodles according to package directions. Heat oil in a large skillet and sauté onion until tender. Add chicken and cook until color changes and chicken is cooked through. Bake almonds in shallow baking dish in oven at 350 degrees for about 10 minutes or until lightly brown. Remove skillet from heat, mix in toasted almonds, salt, and Creamy Cheese Sauce. Add cooked noodles and mix until noodles are thoroughly coated with sauce.

BEEF STROGANOFF

2 teaspoons Aloha Nu Non-Stick Cooking Oil or coconut oil
1 pound beef sirloin cut into 1/4-inch strips
1 medium onion, chopped
4 cloves garlic, minced
4 ounces mushrooms
1 tablespoon tomato paste or 1/4 cup tomato sauce
1 1/2 cups Creamy Cheese Sauce (page 58)
1/2 teaspoon salt
1/8 teaspoon pepper
1 cup plain yogurt or sour cream
Noodles

In a skillet at medium heat add oil and lightly brown both sides of sirloin strips. Add onion, garlic, and mushrooms and cook until tender. Stir in tomato paste, Creamy Cheese Sauce, salt, and pepper. Remove from heat and blend in yogurt or sour cream. Serve over hot noodles.

TUNA NOODLE CASSEROLE

6 ounces pasta
2 tablespoons coconut oil
1/2 medium onion, chopped
4 ounces mushrooms, sliced
1/2 cup peas

1 jar (2 ounces) pimiento
1 teaspoon salt
⅛ teaspoon pepper
1 can (6 ounces) tuna
1½ cups Creamy Cheese Sauce (page 58)
3 slices bread, toasted
2 tablespoons butter
Powdered garlic

Cook pasta according to package directions. Heat oil in large skillet and sauté onions until tender. Add mushrooms, peas, pimiento, salt, and pepper to skillet cover, and cook medium heat for about 5 minutes, stirring occasionally. Mix together tuna, vegetables, cooked pasta, and Creamy Cheese Sauce and pour into a 9x9x2-inch baking dish. Lightly toast 3 slices of bread. Butter bread and sprinkle with garlic powder. Break bread into small pieces and sprinkle on top of casserole. Bake at 425 degrees F for 15 to 20 minutes or until bread crumbs are browned.

ORANGE COCONUT CHICKEN

1 slightly beaten egg
¼ cup orange juice
1 cup flaked coconut
⅓ cup flour or dry bread crumbs
1 teaspoon salt
½ teaspoon paprika
1 teaspoon lemon pepper seasoning
1 3-pound chicken, cut into serving-size pieces

Mix together egg and orange juice. In a separate bowl mix coconut, flour, salt, paprika, and lemon pepper. Dip chicken pieces into orange juice mixture and then into coconut mixture. Place chicken, skin side down, in baking dish. Bake at 400 degrees F for 60 minutes.

SESAME CHICKEN ♥

2 tablespoons sesame seed
¼ cup coconut oil
¾ cup onion, diced
3 garlic cloves, diced
4 to 6 chicken breasts, cut in bite-size pieces
⅓ cup peas
½ teaspoon ginger
1 teaspoon crushed red pepper
½ teaspoon salt
3 tablespoons tamari sauce
6 to 8 ounces noodles

In a skillet at medium heat, toast sesame seeds in coconut oil until lightly browned. Add onion and garlic and cook until tender, stirring occasionally. Add chicken, peas, ginger, red pepper, and salt. Bring to a boil, reduce heat, cover and simmer for 10 minutes, stirring occasionally. Stir in tamari sauce and remove from heat. Cook noodles according to package directions. Drain and stir into chicken mixture, thoroughly coating noodles with sauce.

ALMOND CHICKEN WITH NOODLES

½ cup slivered almonds
¼ cup coconut oil
1 onion, diced
4 garlic cloves, diced
4 to 6 chicken breasts, cut in bite-size pieces
½ head broccoli, cut in bite-size pieces
1½ cups coconut milk
½ teaspoon ginger
½ teaspoon salt
3 tablespoons tamari sauce
6 to 8 ounces noodles

In a skillet over medium heat, toast almonds in coconut oil until lightly browned. Add onion and garlic and cook until tender, stirring occasionally. Add chicken, broccoli, coconut milk, ginger, and salt. Bring to a boil, reduce heat, cover, and simmer for 10 minutes, stirring occasionally. Stir in tamari sauce and remove from heat. Cook noodles according to package directions. Drain and stir into chicken mixture thoroughly coating noodles in sauce.

SHRIMP AND PASTA

Juice of 1 lemon
1 onion, finely chopped
½ bell pepper, finely chopped
4 cloves garlic, diced
1 tablespoon white vinegar
½ teaspoon salt
1 can (14 ounces) coconut milk
¼ cup flour
2 tablespoons tomato paste or ¼ cup tomato sauce
⅛ teaspoon cayenne
1 pound fresh shrimp, shelled and deveined
1 tablespoon fresh cilantro, chopped
6 ounces pasta

Make a marinade with lemon, onion, bell pepper, garlic, vinegar, and salt. Marinate the shrimp for 30 minutes. Blend coconut milk and flour together and put into a saucepan. Add the marinade and shrimp mixture along with the tomato paste and cayenne. Cook over low heat, stirring frequently, for about 10 minutes or until the vegetables are cooked and mixture is slightly thickened. Add shrimp and cilantro, cook for 1 to 2 minutes, and remove from heat. Serve over a bed of hot pasta.

SALMON IN COCONUT CREAM SAUCE ♥

1 to 1½ pounds salmon fillets
1 can (14 ounces) coconut milk
1 tablespoon cornstarch
1 teaspoon curry powder
⅛ teaspoon salt
⅛ teaspoon white pepper
½ cup tomato, chopped
¼ cup fresh cilantro, chopped

Preheat oven to 350 degrees F. Put salmon in a casserole dish. Blend together coconut milk, cornstarch, curry powder, salt, and pepper and pour over salmon. Bake for 1 hour. Serve salmon with the coconut cream sauce garnished with fresh tomato and cilantro. Goes well with a little of the sauce poured on top a side dish of vegetables such as broccoli, green beans, or peas.

FRIED SOLE WITH COCONUT

¼ cup coconut milk
2 tablespoons lime juice
1 teaspoon soy sauce
4 to 6 (4-ounce) sole fillets
¼ cup flour
½ teaspoon ground coriander
½ teaspoon ground cumin
⅛ teaspoon cayenne pepper
½ teaspoon salt
1 tablespoon Aloha Nu Non-Stick Cooking Oil or ¼ cup coconut oil
¼ cup shredded coconut, toasted
2 tablespoons fresh cilantro
Mango, sliced
Lime wedges

Mix coconut milk, lime juice, and soy sauce in small bowl. Arrange fish fillets in large, shallow dish. Pour coconut milk mixture over and let sit for 1 hour.

Mix together flour, coriander, cumin, cayenne pepper, and salt. Remove fish from coconut milk and pat dry. Dredge in flour mixture, shaking off excess. Heat oil in large skillet over medium heat. Cook fish in skillet, turning after about 4 minutes and cook the other side the same amount of time. Remove from heat and place on serving dish. Garnish with toasted coconut and minced cilantro. Serve with sliced mango and lime wedges.

CATFISH IN COCONUT SAUCE

1 pound catfish (2 to 3 fillets)
2 teaspoons Aloha Nu Non-Stick Cooking Oil or 3 tablespoons coconut oil
1 medium onion, sliced
4 cloves garlic, minced
2 medium carrots, sliced
1 cup green beans
1 ½ cups coconut milk
½ teaspoon ground ginger
1 teaspoon salt
¼ teaspoon pepper
2 tablespoons lemon juice
⅓ cup chopped cashews or toasted coconut

In a skillet at medium heat lightly sauté both sides of fish in oil. Add vegetables and cook until crisp and tender, about 5 minutes. Add coconut milk, ginger, salt, and pepper. Cover and simmer for about 10 minutes. Add lemon juice, remove from heat, and garnish with cashews or toasted coconut before serving.

CHICKEN RICE CASSEROLE ♥

¾ cup brown rice
2 tablespoons coconut oil
½ medium onion, chopped
1 stalk celery, chopped
½ bell pepper, chopped
3 to 4 chicken breasts, cut into bite-size pieces*
⅓ cup flour

1½ teaspoons salt
⅛ teaspoon pepper
4 ounces fresh mushroom, chopped
1 can (4 ounces) pimiento
1 cup chicken broth
1 cup coconut milk
1 cup cheese, shredded
Cayenne (optional)

Soak rice in 2¼ cups water for at least 4 hours or overnight. Simmer for 45 minutes or until water is absorbed and rice is tender. Set aside.

Heat coconut oil in a large skillet. Sauté onion, celery, and bell pepper until tender. Add chicken and blend in flour, salt, and pepper. Add mushrooms, pimiento, chicken broth, and coconut milk. Bring to a boil, reduce heat, and simmer, stirring frequently. Cook until mixture thickens slightly and chicken is cooked. Combine mixture with rice and pour into a baking dish. Layer top with shredded cheese and a little cayenne. Cook uncovered in oven at 350 degrees F for 35 minutes. Serves 4.

*You may substitute 1 6-ounce can of tuna for the chicken if you desire.

CHICKEN A LA KING ♥

½ green pepper, chopped
½ onion, chopped
2 tablespoons coconut oil
⅓ cup flour
1 teaspoon salt
¼ teaspoon pepper
1 can (14 ounces) coconut milk
1 cup water or chicken broth
1 can (4 ounces) mushroom stems and pieces, drained
2 to 3 chicken breasts, cut into bite-size pieces
1 jar (4 ounces) pimiento, chopped

Sauté onion and bell pepper in coconut oil until tender. Stir in flour. Add remaining ingredients, bring to a boil, reduce heat, and simmer for 10 minutes. Stir frequently. Serve over hot biscuits, toast, mashed potatoes, rice, or noodles. Makes 6 servings.

Mushroom A La King

Make Chicken A La King following directions but delete the chicken and caned mushroom and use 8 ounces of fresh sliced mushrooms. Mushrooms should be cooked with the onion.

Sausage A La King

Make Chicken A La King according to directions but delete the chicken and add ½ pound of sausage and 1 teaspoon ground sage. Cook sausage with the onion and pepper.

CREAMY CHICKEN AND BISCUITS ❤

½ medium onion, finely chopped
1 stalk celery, finely chopped
2 tablespoons coconut oil
⅓ cup flour
2 to 3 chicken breasts, cut in bite-size pieces
1 cup water or chicken broth
1 can (14 ounces) coconut milk
½ cup peas
1 teaspoon salt
¼ teaspoon pepper
1 teaspoon sage
1 tablespoon butter (optional)
Coconut Milk Biscuits (page 143)

Sauté onion and celery in coconut oil until tender. Stir in flour. Add remaining ingredients, bring to a boil, reduce heat, and simmer for 10 minutes. Stir frequently. Serve over hot biscuits, toast, mashed potatoes, rice, or noodles. Makes 6 servings.

Creamy Tuna and Biscuits

Make above recipe as directed but omit chicken, add 2 cans (6 ounces each) of tuna, and add 1 teaspoon fish sauce. Fish sauce is salty so you will need to reduce the amount of salt added. Fish sauce is available in the Asian section of the grocery store.

HAM AND POTATO CASSEROLE

2 cans (14 ounces each) coconut milk
½ cup water
½ cup flour
1 ½ teaspoons salt
¾ teaspoon pepper
2 tablespoons butter or extra virgin olive oil
5 to 6 potatoes thinly sliced (about 6 cups)
1 medium onion, finely chopped
1 cup ham, finely chopped
2 cups cheese, shredded
Paprika

In a bowl stir together coconut milk, water, flour, salt, and pepper; set aside. Grease bottom of casserole dish with butter or olive oil. Cut potatoes into thin slices. Layer half of the potatoes on the bottom of the casserole dish, followed by half the onion and half of the ham, half of the coconut milk mixture, and top with half of the cheese. Repeat the potato, onion, ham, coconut milk mixture, and cheese layering with the remaining half of the ingredients. Sprinkle top with paprika. Cover and bake at 375 degrees F for 1 hour and 15 minutes. Uncover and bake 15 minutes more.

Spinach Ham and Potato Casserole
Make Ham and Potato Casserole as directed but add 1 10-ounce package of spinach. Thaw spinach and squeeze out all liquid. Evenly layer all of the spinach on the first layer of potatoes.

SHEPHERD'S PIE

1 pound ground beef
½ cup onion, chopped
½ cup bell pepper, chopped
1 cup mushrooms, chopped
1 cup green beans
¼ cup flour

1 can (14 ounces) coconut milk
¼ cup water
1 teaspoon salt
⅛ teaspoon pepper
¼ cup tomato sauce
3 cups hot Creamy Mashed Potatoes (page 123)
1 cup cheese, shredded
Paprika

Preheat oven to 400 degrees F. Brown ground beef in large skillet; add onion, bell pepper, mushrooms, and green beans and cook until tender; stir in flour. Add coconut milk, water, salt, pepper, and tomato sauce. Heat, stirring frequently, until mixture thickens, about 5 minutes. Spoon into an ungreased 1½-quart casserole dish, spread potatoes over surface and roughen with a fork. Sprinkle top with cheese and paprika. Bake uncovered 30 minutes.

COCONUT BATTERED SHRIMP

¾ cup flour
¾ cup water
2 tablespoons tamari sauce
1 egg
½ teaspoon onion powder
½ teaspoon salt
⅛ teaspoon pepper
Coconut oil
½ pound large shrimp, peeled and deveined, with tails left on
2 cups flaked coconut

Mix together flour, water, tamari sauce, egg, onion powder, salt, and pepper. In a deep sauté pan, heat coconut oil to about 325 degrees F. Pick up each shrimp, one at a time, by the tail and dip in the batter, then coat evenly with coconut. Deep fry the shrimp in the hot oil until golden brown, about 3 to 4 minutes. Remove and place on a paper towel. Several shrimp can be cooked at the same time depending on the size of the pan. Season to taste. Goes well with chutney, salsa, or chili sauce.

JUMBO FRIED COCONUT SHRIMP

1 cup flour
3 eggs, beaten
¼ teaspoon cayenne pepper
1 teaspoon onion powder
1 teaspoon salt
3 cups dried bread crumbs
1 cup shredded coconut
24 large shrimp, peeled and deveined, with tails left on
Coconut oil for frying

Place flour in bowl. In a second bowl, combine eggs, cayenne pepper, onion powder, and salt. In a third bowl, mix together bread crumbs and coconut. Holding shrimp by tail, dredge in flour, shaking off excess, then dip into eggs, and finally roll in bread crumb mixture, coating each side. Heat oil in deep fryer or large saucepan to 300 degrees F. Fry shrimp until golden brown, about 3 minutes. Remove and place on paper towel.

AFRICAN COCONUT SHRIMP

¼ cup coconut oil
3 pounds shrimp, peeled, deveined, with tails removed
1 onion, finely chopped
4 garlic cloves, minced
3 springs parsley, finely chopped
2 large tomatoes, chopped
2 teaspoons crushed red pepper
2 teaspoons cumin
1 teaspoon salt
3 cups coconut milk
Hot cooked rice

Heat coconut oil in heavy skillet over medium heat. Cook shrimp until pink. Remove from pan and set aside. In the same pan, sauté onion, garlic, and parsley for 2 to 3 minutes. Add tomatoes, crushed red pepper, cumin, and salt and cook until the mixture thickens slightly, stirring constantly. Reduce heat and add coconut milk and cooked shrimp. Cook and stir until shrimp is heated. Serve over rice.

SHRIMP AND ASPARAGUS IN COCONUT SAUCE

1 medium onion, chopped
1 bell pepper, chopped
3 tablespoons coconut oil
1 pound asparagus, chopped
2 tablespoons flour
1 cup coconut milk
24 large shrimp
2 teaspoons fish sauce*
Salt and pepper

Sauté onion and pepper in oil until tender and onion starts to brown. Add asparagus and cook until tender. Mix flour into coconut milk. Combine coconut milk, shrimp, and fish sauce with vegetables and simmer for about 5 minutes or until shrimp are cooked and sauce begins to thicken. Add salt and pepper to taste.

* Tamari sauce can be substituted for fish sauce if you like.

CHAPTER 7

Asian-Style Cuisine

ASIAN SPICES

Coconuts grow throughout much of Asia where they are extensively used in food preparation and cooking. Many of the classic or traditional foods associated with Thai and Indian cuisine involve coconut in one form or another. This chapter provides a variety of coconut-based meals inspired by traditional Asian dishes. Some of the meals are completely authentic while others are modified for ease of preparation using readily available ingredients.

Asian-style cuisine is characterized by its unique blend of exotic herbs and spices. People in non-Asian countries are often unfamiliar with many of the spices commonly used in Asian cooking, some of which can be hard to find outside their native countries. That isn't a problem with the recipes here. All of the spices and sauces used in this chapter can be found in your local grocery store, usually in the spice section. Some items, such as red curry paste and fish sauce, may be located in the Asian Foods section. Such ingredients are also available at many health food stores and Asian markets. If you can't find them locally, they are available by mail.

Spices and sauces commonly used in Asian cooking that are included in this chapter are listed below.

Herbs and Spices
Curry powder
Lemongrass
Cinnamon
Cardamom
Cloves
Turmeric
Garlic
Coriander
Ginger
Cumin
Mustard
Cayenne pepper
Chili powder
Crushed red pepper
Garam masala
Cilantro

Sauces and Condiments
Red curry paste
Green curry paste
Red chili paste
Fish sauce
Tahini (sesame seed butter)
Chutney

Many Asian dishes are served with rice. Long-grain basmati rice is one of the most popular. I prefer short-grain brown rice. All of the dishes in this chapter may be made with any type of rice you prefer.

In Thailand, noodle dishes are popular. The most common noodles used in Thai cooking are rice noodles made from white rice flour. A variety of noodles made with other grains are also available, such as brown rice, whole wheat, corn, and spelt. You can use any of these noodles in the recipes that follow.

Fish sauce is the most popular seasoning in Thai cooking. It is made by extracting the juice from salted anchovies and is used much as you would use soy sauce. Because of its high salt content, additional salt is usually not needed. It has a pungent taste and aroma, which mellows when cooked. It adds a nice flavor to shrimp and other seafood dishes. If fish sauce is not available, you can generally substitute soy or tamari sauce.

Other common flavorings in Thai cooking are red or green curry paste and red chili paste. They can greatly enhance the flavor of foods. These pastes are hot, so be careful how much you use. If you put too much in a dish, you can temper the hotness by adding at little milk or yogurt.

Some Thai dishes are often called curries, but Indian food is characterized by its many flavorful and aromatic curries. Curries may contain any number or combination of seasonings including garam masala or curry powder. Curry is a term that has been applied to Asian, and particularly Indian, foods to describe any main dish or stew. Many curries contain no curry powder at all, yet they are still called curries. Curry powder isn't made from any single herb but is actually a blend of several different Indian spices such as coriander, turmeric, chili, cumin, and fenugreek. It is the turmeric that gives curry powder its distinctive mustard yellow color. Garam masala, like curry powder, is made from a blend of different spices including coriander, black pepper, cumin, cardamom, and cinnamon. Curries may or may not contain curry powder or garam masala.

THAI CHICKEN

1 3- to 4-inch hot red finger pepper (or other hot pepper)
2 tablespoons coconut oil
1 large clove garlic, minced
1 ½-inch piece ginger root, minced
1 medium onion, sliced
1 red bell pepper, sliced
1 green bell pepper, sliced
1 tablespoon minced lemon grass (about 3 inches)
1½ pounds boneless chicken breast
1 tablespoon fish sauce
½ cup coconut milk
¼ teaspoon red curry paste
Salt to taste

Remove seeds from hot red pepper and mince. Heat coconut oil in large skillet. Add minced garlic, ginger, and minced hot red pepper; sauté for 2 minutes. Add onion and cook another 2 minutes. Add red and green peppers and lemon grass; cook 2 minutes. Cut chicken breasts in half and slice halves into ½-inch slices, add to skillet along with fish sauce. Cook on medium-low heat for about 10 minutes, stirring frequently until chicken becomes white and firm. Stir in coconut milk and curry paste, add salt to taste, cook until heated.

INDIAN-STYLE LAMB STEW
This thick stew can be served on a plate rather than in a bowl.

1 small onion, chopped
6 cloves garlic, chopped
2 medium carrots, sliced
1 bell pepper, chopped
2 tablespoons coconut oil
3 tablespoons flour
2 cups water
1 can (14 ounces) coconut milk

1 ½ pounds lamb, cut into bite-size pieces
3 to 4 medium potatoes, chopped
¼ teaspoon cinnamon
1 teaspoon cardamom
¼ teaspoon ground cloves
½ teaspoon ground turmeric
1 teaspoon coriander
¼ teaspoon cayenne pepper
2 teaspoons salt

Sauté onion, garlic, carrots, and bell pepper in coconut oil until vegetables are tender. Mix flour with water; combine the water, coconut milk, lamb, potatoes, and spices with the meat and vegetables; bring to a boil, reduce heat, and simmer for about 20 minutes until potatoes are tender; stir occasionally.

Variations
Instead of lamb you can make this dish using chicken, pork, or shrimp.

CHICKEN IN CURRY SAUCE

4 tablespoons coconut oil
2 medium onions, thinly sliced
2 tablespoons flour
1 teaspoon peeled, minced fresh ginger (or ½ teaspoon ground ginger)
1 teaspoon minced garlic
3 pounds raw chicken, cut into small serving size pieces
1 tablespoon curry powder
½ teaspoon ground cumin
½ teaspoon ground coriander
1 teaspoon salt
½ teaspoon pepper
1 can (14 ounces) coconut milk
¼ cup chutney
½ cup raisins
½ cup roasted cashews
3 scallions, thinly sliced

In large frying pan with tight-fitting lid, heat coconut oil over medium heat. Add onions and cook, uncovered, until tender, about 4 minutes. Add flour, ginger, and garlic and continue cooking 4 minutes, stirring occasionally, until softened. Add chicken pieces and cook until evenly browned, turning once or twice, about 8 minutes. In medium bowl, combine curry powder, cumin, coriander, salt, pepper, coconut milk, and chutney and stir well. Scrape mixture into frying pan and turn chicken and onion to combine well. Reduce heat to low, cover and simmer, turning chicken once or twice, until it is tender and cooked through, about 45 minutes. Stir in raisins and cashews, transfer to serving dish and sprinkle with scallions. Serve with a side dish of rice.

CHICKEN AND VEGETABLES IN CREAM SAUCE

This is a slightly modified version of a popular Indian recipe. A vegetarian version can be made by simply omitting the chicken. Green chili peppers give this dish a bit of a kick, which adds to the flavor. You can decrease the hotness of the dish by adjusting the number and type of peppers you use.

⅔ cup plain yogurt
¼ cup tomato sauce
2 tablespoons lemon juice
1 teaspoon ground ginger
1 teaspoon chili powder
1 teaspoon ground coriander
1 teaspoon ground cumin
1 teaspoon dry mustard
1 teaspoon salt
2 tablespoons peanut butter or tahini
⅓ cup water
⅓ cup coconut oil
½ cup onion, chopped
4 cloves garlic, diced
1 to 4 hot chili peppers (depending how hot you want it)
8 to 10 cauliflower flowerets
1 carrot, sliced
4 small potatoes, cubed (about 2 cups)
4 chicken breasts, cut into bite-size pieces
3 tablespoons flour
1 cup coconut milk
1 cup water
2 tablespoons fresh cilantro, chopped
½ cup cottage cheese

Mix together yogurt, tomato sauce, lemon juice, ginger, chili powder, coriander, cumin, mustard, salt, peanut butter, and ⅓ cup water. Set aside.

Heat coconut oil in large skillet. Add onion and cook until slightly tender. Add garlic, chili peppers, cauliflower, carrot, and potatoes, cover and cook for about 10 minutes until potatoes are tender, stirring occasionally. Add chicken, cover, and cook 5 minutes. Remove cooked vegetables and chicken from pan with a slotted spoon and set aside.

Stir flour into the remaining oil in the skillet and cook until slightly browned. Pour in the yogurt and spice mixture, coconut milk, and 1 cup water. Cook for 5 minutes, stirring constantly until the sauce comes to a boil and begins to thicken. Return the cooked vegetables and chicken to the pan, stirring gently to blend into the sauce. Stir in cilantro and cottage cheese. Cook for about 2 minutes.

POTATOES AND GREEN BEANS
IN COCONUT SAUCE ♥

In India this dish is called Aloo Phalli. Like many Indian curries, this recipe does not contain "curry." Curry is a term used in the west to describe any type of Indian stew or main dish. One of the primary flavorings used in this recipe is garam masala. Garam masala is a combination of spices popularly used in Indian cooking. Like many Indian dishes this one can be made with or without meat. This recipe includes chicken, but you can leave it out if you want. It makes a delightful vegetarian dish.

1 cup plain yogurt
½ cup coconut milk
1 ½ teaspoons garam masala
1 teaspoon chili powder
1 teaspoon ground ginger
¼ teaspoon turmeric
¼ teaspoon cumin
¼ teaspoon ground cardamom
2 teaspoons salt
⅓ cup coconut oil
1 medium onion, chopped
4 cloves garlic, diced
3 to 4 medium potatoes, chopped

½ cup green beans, sliced
½ cauliflower, cut into flowerets
½ bell pepper, chopped
4 chicken breasts, cut into bite-size pieces
¾ cup cashews
2 tablespoons flour
1 tablespoon fresh cilantro, chopped

Mix together yogurt, coconut milk, garam masala, chili powder, ginger, turmeric, cumin, cardamom, and salt. Set aside.

Heat coconut oil in large skillet and sauté onion until tender. Add garlic, potatoes, green beans, cauliflower, and bell pepper. Cook about 10 minutes, stirring occasionally. Add chicken, cashews, and flour. Cover and cook 3 minutes. Stir in yogurt mixture. Continue to cook, stirring occasionally, until vegetables are tender. Add cilantro and cook 1 additional minute.

Like many curries, this dish goes well served with a side dish of fresh fruit.

SHRIMP AND CAULIFLOWER IN COCONUT SAUCE

⅓ cup coconut oil
1 medium onion, chopped
½ cup slivered almonds
1 teaspoon ground coriander
2 teaspoons ginger
2 teaspoons curry powder
1 teaspoon salt
2 tablespoons flour
4 cloves garlic, minced
1 to 3 chili peppers, chopped
½ cauliflower, cut into small flowerets
1 bell pepper, chopped
3 cups shrimp
1 can (14 ounces) coconut milk
2 tablespoons cilantro, chopped

Heat coconut oil in a large skillet and sauté onion until tender. Add almonds and cook for 4 or 5 minutes. Add spices and flour and cook, stirring occasionally, for 4 minutes. Stir in garlic, chili pepper, cauliflower, and bell pepper, cover and cook until vegetables are tender. Add shrimp, coconut milk, and cilantro. Stir constantly until sauce thickens and shrimp is cooked.

POTATO AND PEA KORMA ♥

This is a delicious meatless dish from India. If desired, you could add chicken for a non-vegetarian version.

½ cup plain yogurt
1 cup coconut milk
1 tablespoon lemon juice
½ cup tomato sauce
1 teaspoon salt
1 teaspoon garam masala
1 teaspoon ground ginger
1 ½ teaspoons ground coriander
1 teaspoon chili powder
½ teaspoon ground cardamom
⅛ teaspoon black pepper
½ teaspoon ground cinnamon
⅓ cup coconut oil
2 tablespoons sesame seeds
1 large onion, chopped
4 garlic cloves, chopped
2 to 3 potatoes, cubed
½ cup green beans, sliced
½ cup peas
2 tomatoes
2 tablespoons fresh cilantro, chopped

Mix together yogurt, coconut milk, lemon juice, tomato sauce, salt, and all the spices and set aside. Heat coconut oil in a large skillet. Add sesame seeds and onion and sauté until onions are tender. Add garlic, potatoes, green beans, and peas. Cook for about 10 minutes stirring occasionally. Stir in yogurt mixture and simmer until potatoes are tender, but not mushy. Cut each tomato into about 10 or 12 wedges. Add the tomato wedges and cilantro to skillet and cook 1 minute. Remove from heat and serve. This dish goes well served with a side dish of fried okra (page 130).

For the non-vegetarian version, add 4 chicken breasts cut into bite-size pieces. Put the chicken to the skillet along with the yogurt and cook as directed.

PINEAPPLE SHRIMP IN COCONUT MILK

2 cups cauliflower, sliced
1 medium carrot, sliced
½ cup onion, chopped
2 tablespoons coconut oil
2 tablespoons flour
1 can (14 ounces) coconut milk
1 teaspoon salt
⅛ teaspoon pepper
1 tablespoon ground ginger
½ pound medium-size shrimp, shelled
1 ½ cup pineapple chunks
Hot cooked rice

In a large saucepan, sauté cauliflower, carrot, and onion in coconut oil until tender. Add flour and cook 1 minute. Add coconut milk, salt, pepper, and ginger. Reduce heat to low and simmer for 10 minutes Increase heat to high and add the shrimp. Cook for 1 minute or until shrimp turn pink. Add pineapple and cook 1 minute. Remove from heat. Serve over hot cooked rice.

PEANUT CHICKEN

1 tablespoon coconut oil
1 ½ pounds chicken, cut into 1-inch pieces
1 onion, chopped
1 red bell pepper, chopped
1 medium zucchini, sliced
1 tablespoon flour
1 can (14 ounces) coconut milk
1 lemon, juiced
½ cup salsa
1 tablespoon red chili paste
1 teaspoon salt

¾ cup chunky peanut butter
Hot cooked rice

Heat oil in a large skillet. Add chicken, onion, bell pepper, and zucchini; cook until vegetables are tender. Stir in flour. Add coconut milk, lemon juice, salsa, chili paste, salt, and peanut butter. Reduce heat and simmer for 10 minutes. Serve over hot cooked rice.

APPLE AND SWEET POTATO CURRY

This recipe can serve as a vegetarian main course or as a great side dish.

1 medium sweet potato or yam, cut in bite-size pieces
1 medium onion, chopped
3 tablespoons coconut oil
1 teaspoon ground mustard
1½ teaspoon ground cumin
1 teaspoon ground coriander
½ teaspoon turmeric
1 teaspoon salt
2 cloves garlic, minced
2 tart apples, peeled, seeded, and sliced
½ cup raisins
1 can (14 ounces) coconut milk
¼ cup flaked or shredded coconut

Sauté onion in coconut oil until tender. Add spices and cook 2 minutes. Stir in remaining ingredients, cover, and simmer until sweet potato is tender.

CHICKEN IN RED CURRY SAUCE

¼ cup coconut oil
4 to 6 chicken thighs, boned and halved
3 tablespoons red curry paste
2 cups water
1 can (14 ounces) coconut milk
1 sweet potato, cut in bite-size pieces
¼ cup fresh cilantro, chopped

Place coconut oil and chicken in skillet on medium heat. Cover and cook chicken for 5 minutes, turn and cook another 5 minutes. Add red curry paste, water, coconut milk, and sweet potato. Cover and simmer for about 15 minutes or until sweet potato is tender and sauce is thickened. Uncover, add cilantro, and cook for 2 minutes.

THAI COCONUT SHRIMP AND NOODLES ❤

8 ounces noodles
1 cup onion, chopped
3 tablespoons coconut oil
2 tablespoons green chili, chopped
4 cloves garlic, minced
1 tablespoon flour
1 can (14 ounces) coconut milk
2 tablespoons fish sauce
½ pound shrimp, peeled and deveined
2 tablespoons fresh cilantro, finely chopped

Prepare noodles according to package directions, drain, and set aside. Traditionally rice noodles are most commonly used in Thai cooking, but you can use any type of noodle you like.

In a large skillet, sauté onions in coconut oil until tender. Add green chili, garlic, and flour and continue to cook for 3 minutes, stirring frequently. Stir in coconut milk and fish sauce and simmer uncovered for about 8 minutes until sauce thickens. Stir occasionally. Add shrimp and cilantro and continue to simmer until shrimp is cooked, about 3 to 4 minutes. Remove from heat and fold in noodles until well coated with sauce. Serve hot.

RED THAI CURRY

1 pound noodles
2 tablespoons coconut oil
1 onion, chopped
4 garlic cloves, minced
2 carrots, sliced
1 red bell pepper, diced

1 tablespoon ground ginger
1 tablespoon flour
1 can (14 ounces) coconut milk
1 tablespoon red curry paste*
2 tablespoons fish sauce or soy sauce
1 pound shrimp, peeled and deveined
¼ cup cilantro, finely chopped

Prepare noodles according to package directions, drain, and set aside. Heat oil in skillet and sauté onion and garlic until tender. Add carrots, bell pepper, and ginger and sauté until vegetables are soft, about 7 minutes. Mix flour into coconut milk. Add coconut milk, curry paste, and fish sauce to skillet and cook until curry paste is well blended. Add shrimp, reduce heat and simmer 3 to 4 minutes or until shrimp are pink. Remove from heat and fold in noodles until well coated with sauce. Garnish with cilantro.

*Red curry paste is hot. You may adjust spiciness of this dish by adding or reducing the amount of curry paste used. If you find you have used too much, you can reduce the hotness by adding a little milk or yogurt.

LAMB AND SQUASH CURRY

¼ cup coconut oil
1 onion, chopped
4 cloves garlic, chopped
1 large zucchini or yellow squash, sliced
2 potatoes, cubed
1 carrot, sliced
1 fresh green chili, chopped
1 pound lamb, cubed*
2 tablespoons ground coriander
1 tablespoon chili powder
1 teaspoon ground cumin
1 teaspoon ground ginger
1 teaspoon turmeric
2 teaspoons curry powder
1 tablespoon ground mustard
2 teaspoons salt
1 cup water

3 tablespoons flour
1 can (14 ounces) coconut milk
¼ cup apple cider vinegar

Heat coconut oil in a large skillet and sauté onion and garlic until tender. Add squash, potatoes, carrot, and green chili, cover and cook for 5 to 7 minutes stirring occasionally. Add meat, all spices, salt, and water and simmer until potatoes are tender. Mix flour into coconut milk and add to skillet along with vinegar. Cook until mixture thickens.

* Pork may be substituted for lamb if you wish.

GINGERED SWEET POTATOES
IN COCONUT SAUCE ♥
This recipe makes a good meatless main course or side dish.

3 tablespoons coconut oil
1 onion, diced
1 tablespoon ground ginger
1 tablespoon curry powder
1 can (14 ounces) coconut milk
1 large sweet potato, cut in bite-size pieces
1 cup pineapple, chopped
1 tablespoon tamari sauce
1 teaspoon salt

Heat coconut oil in a large saucepan. Sauté onion until tender. Mix in ginger and curry powder and cook for another 1 to 2 minutes until fragrant. Add coconut milk, sweet potatoes, pineapple, tamari sauce, and salt. Reduce heat to low, cover, and simmer for 25 to 30 minutes, until sweet potatoes are soft but still firm enough to keep their shape.

POTATO AND SPINACH CURRY

3 tablespoons coconut oil
4 red potatoes, diced
1 onion, chopped

4 cloves garlic, minced
1 can (14 ounces) coconut milk
1 tablespoon ground ginger
1 teaspoon ground cumin
2 teaspoons ground turmeric
2 teaspoons salt
1 10-ounce package of frozen chopped spinach*
1 large tomato, diced
¼ cup cilantro, minced

Heat coconut oil in a large skillet. At medium heat, cover and cook potatoes, onion, and garlic for 10 minutes. Reduce heat; add coconut milk, ginger, cumin, turmeric, and salt; simmer until potatoes are tender but still hold their shape, about 10 minutes. Add spinach and tomato and cook for 2 minutes longer. Serve garnished with cilantro.

*One pound of fresh spinach can be substituted for frozen if desired.

PEANUT BUTTER PORK

1 cup coconut milk
½ cup chunky peanut butter
1 tablespoon red chili paste
1 tablespoon lemon juice
1 teaspoon ground ginger
1 teaspoon salt
2 tablespoons coconut oil
1 medium onion, chopped
2 garlic cloves, diced
½ red bell pepper, diced
1 pound pork, cut into bite-size pieces
Noodles

Combine coconut milk, peanut butter, red chili paste, lemon juice, ginger, and salt. Mix together and set aside. Heat coconut oil in large skillet. Sauté pork until it is barely cooked through, about 4 minutes. Add onions, garlic, and bell pepper and continue to cook until vegetables are tender and meat is thoroughly cooked. Stir in coconut milk mixture, reduce heat and simmer for 4 or 5 minutes. Serve over a bed of hot noodles.

COCONUT SEAFOOD STEW ♥

1 ½ cups chicken broth or water
½ onion, diced
1 potato, chopped
8-ounce fresh fish fillet*
1 10-ounce package spinach
¼ teaspoon ground ginger
½ teaspoon coriander
1 ½ teaspoons fish sauce
½ teaspoon green curry paste
1 can (14 ounces) coconut milk
¼ teaspoon salt
8 ounces shrimp
Juice of half a lime

Heat chicken broth or water in a large saucepan. Add onion, potato, and fish fillet with the skin on and simmer for about 10 minutes. Remove fish fillet. Add spinach, ginger, coriander, fish sauce, green curry paste, coconut milk, and salt and simmer for 10 minutes or until potato is tender. Remove skin from fish fillet and cut or break fish into ½-inch pieces. Add fish and shrimp to the saucepan and cook another 3 minutes until shrimp is cooked. Remove from heat and add lime juice. Serve in bowls.

*You can use any type of white fish.

COCONUT CHICKEN SOUP ♥

4 cups water
½ medium onion, chopped
3 cloves garlic, chopped
3 chicken breasts, cut into bite-size pieces
1 large tomato, chopped
1 ½ tablespoons fish sauce
1 teaspoon curry powder
1 teaspoon ground ginger
1 teaspoon salt
1 can (14 ounces) coconut milk

1 pound fresh spinach, chopped*
¼ cup cilantro, chopped

Bring water to a boil in a large saucepan. Add onion, garlic, chicken, tomato, fish sauce, curry powder, ginger, and salt. Reduce heat, cover, and simmer for 15 minutes. Add coconut milk and spinach and cook additional 5 minutes. Remove from heat and add cilantro.

*One 10-ounce package of frozen chopped spinach can be substituted for fresh spinach if desired.

CHICKEN AND SWEET POTATO STEW WITH COCONUT DUMPLINGS

4 cups chicken broth
3 chicken breasts, cut into bite-size pieces
½ onion, chopped
6 cloves garlic, chopped
1 medium sweet potato, chopped (3 cups)
1 cup peas
1½ teaspoons salt
2 teaspoons curry powder
½ teaspoon garam masala
1 teaspoon ground cardamom
⅛ teaspoon pepper
1 tablespoon flour
1 can (14 ounces) coconut milk
Coconut Dumplings (below)

In a large saucepan, bring chicken broth to a boil. Add chicken, onion, garlic, sweet potato, peas, salt, and spices. Reduce heat and simmer for 20 minutes or until sweet potato is barely tender. Mix flour into coconut milk and stir into stew. Drop Coconut Dumplings into stew, cover, and simmer for 15 minutes. Serve in bowls.

Coconut Dumplings
1 cup flour
½ cup grated coconut

120

½ teaspoon onion powder
¼ cup cilantro, diced
½ teaspoon salt
1 ½ teaspoons baking powder
½ cup coconut milk
1 large egg

Mix flour, coconut, onion powder, cilantro, salt, and baking powder together. In a separate bowl mix coconut milk and egg together. Combine the wet and dry ingredients. Form the dough into 1-inch balls. Coat each one in flour and drop into stew.

BURMESE PEANUT CHICKEN

1 chicken (3 to 4 pounds), cut into serving-size pieces
2 teaspoons Aloha Nu Non-Stick Cooking Oil or 3 tablespoons coconut oil
1 medium yellow onion, chopped
1 carrot, sliced
1 celery stalk, sliced
3 garlic cloves, minced
¼ teaspoon cinnamon
½ teaspoon ginger
Dash of cayenne pepper
⅛ teaspoon cloves
1 teaspoon salt
3 tablespoons soy sauce
½ cup chunky peanut butter
1 can (14 ounces) coconut milk
Hot cooked rice

In a heavy skillet at medium heat, brown chicken well on all sides in oil. Add onion, carrot, celery, and garlic and cook until slightly tender. Mix in spices, salt, soy sauce, peanut butter, and coconut milk, cover, and simmer for 20 minutes or until chicken is done. Serve over hot cooked rice.

CHAPTER 8

Side Dishes

CREAMY SCALLOPED POTATOES

1 can (14 ounces) coconut milk
½ cup water
¼ cup flour
2 teaspoons salt
¼ teaspoon pepper
4 to 6 potatoes thinly sliced
1 medium onion, finely chopped
1 red or green bell pepper, chopped
2 cups cheese, grated
Paprika

In a bowl stir together coconut milk, water, flour, salt, and pepper; set aside. Grease bottom of casserole dish with coconut oil or butter. Cut potatoes into thin slices. Layer half of the potatoes on the bottom of the casserole, followed by half of the onion, bell pepper, cheese, and coconut milk mixture. Repeat the potato, onion, bell pepper, cheese, and coconut milk mixture, layering with the remaining half of the ingredients. Sprinkle top with paprika. Bake at 350 degrees F for 1 hour and 15 minutes, or until potatoes are tender.

CREAMY MASHED POTATOES

2 pounds potatoes (about 6 medium)
⅓ to ½ cup coconut milk
½ teaspoon salt
Dash of pepper

Chop potatoes into ½-inch pieces and put into pot. Add just enough water to cover potatoes. Cover, heat to boiling, and cook until tender, about 25 to 30 minutes. Drain. Mash potatoes, adding coconut milk a little at a time until smooth and fluffy. (The amount of coconut milk needed depends on the variety of potato.) Add salt and pepper to taste. Makes 4 to 6 servings.

Garlic Mashed Potatoes

Cook potatoes as directed above. After draining water, add 6 to 10 cloves of crushed garlic, ½ teaspoon onion powder, salt, and pepper. Mix ingredients, cover, and let stand for 5 minutes. Mash with enough coconut milk for good consistency. Before serving, sprinkle with paprika or chives if desired.

Lemon Mashed Potatoes

Make Creamy Mashed Potatoes as directed. Stir in 1 tablespoon lemon juice when adding the salt and pepper.

Mexican Mashed Potatoes

Make Creamy Mashed Potatoes as directed. Stir ½ cup salsa into mashed potatoes.

Cheesy Mashed Potatoes

Make Creamy Mashed Potatoes as directed. Stir 1 cup of Thick Cheddar Cheese Sauce (page 58) into mashed potatoes. Sprinkle top with paprika.

Bacon and Cheese Potatoes

Make Creamy Mashed Potatoes as directed. Serve with Creamy Cheese Sauce (page 58) poured over potatoes like gravy and topped with crumbled bacon.

Fried Mashed Potatoes

This is a good way to use leftover mashed potatoes. Combine 1 cup cold mashed potatoes, 1 slightly beaten egg, ¼ cup diced onion, ½ teaspoon salt, and ¼ teaspoon pepper. Mix well. Shape into 6 patties. Heat 2 tablespoons of coconut oil in skillet. Cook at medium high heat, browning each side. Makes 6 servings.

SUPER BAKED POTATO

Scrub potato well and pierce several times with a fork or sharp knife so steam can escape. Bake directly on oven racks at 400 degrees F for 1 hour. Cut potato lengthwise in half. Top with Thick Cheddar Cheese Sauce or Tex-Mex Cheddar Cheese Sauce (page 58), salt and pepper, diced scallions, and crumbled bacon. May also add a little dill, basil, parsley, or marjoram.

TWICE BAKED POTATO ♥

Prepare and bake potato as described above. Remove potato from oven and let cool. As soon as it is cool enough to handle, cut the potato in half lengthwise. Scoop out the center without damaging the skin, leaving a thin shell. Mash the scooped out portion of the potato along with ½ cup of Thick Cheddar Cheese Sauce (pages 58), 1 tablespoon lemon juice, ¼ teaspoon salt, and a dash of pepper for each potato prepared. Blend all the ingredients together

124

until mixture becomes creamy. Mound the mixture into each half of the potato shell. Return to oven and cook at 450 degrees F for 15 minutes or until the top of the potato filling begins to turn brown. Remove from oven and serve. Top with chopped chives or scallions.

Variation

Make as directed but replace the Thick Cheddar Cheese Sauce with Cheese and Shrimp Sauce (page 58)

MASHED SWEET POTATO

1 large sweet potato, cooked*
1 cup coconut milk
1 tart apple, peeled and chopped
2 tablespoons honey or maple syrup
1½ teaspoons cinnamon
¼ teaspoon nutmeg
½ teaspoon salt

Cook sweet potato until soft. Combine coconut milk, apple, honey, cinnamon, nutmeg, and salt in a saucepan. Simmer for about 5 minutes; do not boil. Remove and discard potato skin; mash thoroughly. Mix mashed sweet potato with coconut milk mixture. Serve hot. Garnish with toasted coconut or almonds.

*You may substitute 1 medium butternut squash for the sweet potato if desired.

CREAMED CORN

½ medium onion, chopped
½ cup bell pepper
3 tablespoons butter
2 tablespoons flour
1 can (14 ounces) coconut milk
3 cups corn
1 teaspoon salt
¼ teaspoon pepper

Sauté onion and bell pepper in butter until vegetables are tender. Stir in flour and cook 2 minutes. Add coconut milk, corn, salt, and pepper. Bring to a boil, reduce heat, and simmer until mixture thickens.

CREAMED PEAS

½ medium onion, chopped
2 tablespoons butter
2 tablespoons flour
1 can (14 ounces) coconut milk
2½ cups peas
½ teaspoon salt
¼ teaspoon pepper

Sauté onion in butter until tender. Stir in flour and cook 2 minutes. Add coconut milk, peas, salt, and pepper. Bring to a boil, reduce heat, and simmer until mixture thickens.

Curried Peas

Make Creamed Peas as directed and add 1 teaspoon curry powder.

CREAMED VEGETABLES WITH FISH SAUCE

½ medium onion, chopped
2 tablespoons butter or coconut oil
2 tablespoons flour
1 can (14 ounces) coconut milk
3 cups vegetables
½ teaspoon fish sauce
Salt and pepper to taste

Sauté onion in butter until tender. Stir in flour and cook 2 minutes. Add coconut milk, vegetables, fish sauce, salt, and pepper. Bring to a boil, reduce heat, and simmer until mixture thickens and vegetables are tender. You can use any one of the following vegetables or any combination of them: asparagus, carrots, peas, green beans, broccoli, Brussels sprouts, cauliflower, lima beans, corn, and zucchini.

SPICY CREAMED SPINACH

1 tablespoon coconut oil
½ large onion, finely diced
½ teaspoon ground cumin
¼ teaspoon ground cardamom
¼ teaspoon ground turmeric
¼ teaspoon ground ginger
½ teaspoon salt
10 ounces spinach
½ cup coconut milk

Heat coconut oil in a large skillet. Add onion and cook until tender. Add spices and cook for about 1 minute. Add spinach, cover, and cook for 1 to 2 minutes until slightly wilted. Pour in coconut milk and cook uncovered until spinach is completely cooked, but do not overcook. Serve hot.

CARDAMOM RICE

1 cup brown rice
1 cup water
1 can (14 ounces) coconut milk
½ teaspoon ground cardamom
¼ teaspoon ground cinnamon
¼ teaspoon salt

Soak rice in a saucepan with water for at least 4 hours. Add all remaining ingredients. Bring to a boil, reduce heat, cover, and simmer for 45 minutes or until rice is tender and liquid is absorbed. Goes well with fish, lamb, or chicken.

SESAME ZUCCHINI ♥

2 tablespoons sesame seed
¼ cup coconut oil
½ cup onion, diced
2 garlic cloves, diced
2 medium zucchini, sliced

¼ teaspoon ginger
½ teaspoon salt
2 tablespoons tamari sauce

In a skillet at medium heat, toast sesame seeds in coconut oil until lightly browned. Add onion and garlic and cook for 3 to 4 minutes, stirring occasionally. Add zucchini, cover, and cook until tender. Mix in ginger and salt. Remove from heat and add tamari sauce. Include some of the drippings from pan with each serving.

VEGETABLES WITH CHEESE SAUCE
Make the Creamy Cheese Sauce (page 58) and pour over steamed or sautéed vegetables. Tastes great with asparagus, broccoli, cauliflower, zucchini, Brussels sprouts, potatoes, onions, peas, or bell peppers.

MACARONI AND CHEESE

3 cups cooked elbow macaroni
1 ½ cups Creamy Cheese Sauce (page 58)
1 tablespoon fresh chives, finely chopped

Cook macaroni according to package directions. Drain water from macaroni and mix in Creamy Cheese Sauce. Garnish with fresh chives.

Beef Macaroni and Cheese
In a skillet cook ½ pound of ground beef and ½ medium onion. Mix into the Macaroni and Cheese recipe described above.

Shrimp Macaroni and Cheese
Make the Macaroni and Cheese recipe according to directions but substitute Shrimp Cheese Sauce for Creamy Cheese Sauce.

CHEESE CUPS ♥
This delicious bread pudding is filled with cheese and bacon. Makes a great breakfast or side dish at dinner. The Fruit Cup described below is suitable for breakfast or as an after dinner dessert.

128

3 strips bacon
1 egg
½ cup coconut milk
½ cup flour
¼ teaspoon salt
½ cup Creamy Cheese Sauce (page 58)
Chives

Cook bacon until crisp and set aside, but reserve drippings. Preheat oven to 425 degrees F. In a blender mix egg, coconut milk, flour, and salt at high speed for about 1 minute, until mixture is bubbly. Coat the bottom of a 6-cup muffin pan generously with bacon drippings. Pour egg mixture into cups and bake for 18 minutes. Remove from oven. Each pudding cup will have a slight depression in the center, generously fill with warm Creamy Cheese Sauce and top with crumbled bacon and chives. Serve hot.

Crab Cups
Make Cheese Cups as directed but replace the Creamy Cheese Sauce with Cheese and Crab Sauce (page 58). Garnish with chives.

Shrimp Cups
Make Cheese Cups as directed but replace the Creamy Cheese Sauce with Cheese and Shrimp Sauce (page 58).

Fruit Cups
Make Cheese Cups as directed but omit the bacon, coat muffin pan with coconut oil or butter, and replace the Creamy Cheese Sauce with a Fruit Sauce (page 56).

ONION FRITTERS ♥

1 cup coconut milk
¼ cup water
1 egg
¾ cup flour
1 teaspoon onion powder
½ teaspoon salt
1 large Spanish or Bermuda onion, chopped
Coconut oil

Mix coconut milk, water, egg, flour, onion powder, and salt together until smooth. Chop onion into small pieces and stir into batter. Heat oil in deep fryer or large saucepan to 325 to 350 degrees F. Drop batter by the spoonful into hot oil. Fry a few spoonfuls at a time in hot oil until golden brown. Drain on paper towels. Sprinkle with salt while still hot. Keep warm in hot (200 degree F) oven until ready to serve.

Fried Vegetables

Follow directions for making Onion Fritters but substitute other vegetables for the onion. Vegetables that fry well include okra, cauliflower, carrot, mushroom, zucchini, and yam.

FRENCH FRIES

Peel and cut potatoes lengthwise into thin strips. Fill deep fryer or large saucepan ½ full with coconut oil and heat to 325 to 350 degrees F. Fry potato strips a few at a time until lightly golden and insides are tender. Drain on paper towels. Sprinkle with salt while still hot. Keep warm in hot (200 degree F) oven until ready to serve.

CHEESE NACHOS
Great tasting Cheese Nachos can be made using Coconut Tortilla Corn Chips (below) and Tex-Mex Cheddar Cheese Sauce (page 58). Just pour the cheese sauce over the corn chips and enjoy. Also tastes good combined with ground beef and/or refried beans.

Coconut Tortilla Corn Chips
Fill deep fryer or large saucepan ½ full with coconut oil and heat to 325 to 350 degrees F. Cut each corn tortilla into four equal size pieces. Cook in hot oil for about 2 minutes. Place on a paper towel to drain. Sprinkle fried tortilla with a pinch of salt while still hot.

CHAPTER 9

Breads and Grains

COCONUT BRAN MUFFINS

1 cup water
1 tablespoon vanilla
⅓ cup honey
1 egg
¼ cup wheat bran
1 cup whole wheat flour
¼ cup grated coconut
2 teaspoons baking powder
¼ teaspoon salt
1 teaspoon cinnamon
½ teaspoon nutmeg
¼ cup coconut oil
½ cup nuts

Combine water, vanilla, honey, egg, and bran in a bowl and let sit for about 10 minutes. The bran will absorb some of the moisture as it sits, which will improve the texture of the final product. In another bowl, mix flour, grated coconut, baking powder, salt, cinnamon, and nutmeg. Preheat oven to 400 degrees F. Add melted (not hot) coconut oil to the liquid ingredients, add the nuts and mix together. Combine the wet and dry ingredients into one bowl and mix just until moist. Do not over mix or the muffins will not rise as well. Coat muffin cups with non-stick cooking oil (page 7) or coconut oil. Fill muffins cups half full. Bake for 15 minutes. Makes one dozen muffins.

COCONUTTY MUFFINS

1 cup water
1 teaspoon vanilla
½ teaspoon almond extract
⅓ cup honey
1 egg
1 cup whole wheat flour
½ cup grated coconut
2 teaspoons baking powder
¼ teaspoon salt
¼ cup coconut oil
½ cup nuts (almonds, pecans, or walnuts)

Combine water, vanilla, almond extract, honey, and egg, in a bowl and set aside. In another bowl mix flour, grated coconut, baking powder, and salt. Preheat oven to 400 degrees F. Add melted (not hot) coconut oil to the liquid ingredients, add the nuts and mix together. Combine the wet and dry ingredients into one bowl and mix just until moist. Coat muffin cups with non-stick cooking oil (page 7) or coconut oil. Fill muffins cups half full. Bake for 15 minutes. Makes one dozen muffins.

BLUEBERRY COCONUT MUFFINS

½ cup coconut milk
1 egg
½ cup honey
1 teaspoon vanilla
1 cup whole wheat flour
½ cup grated coconut
2 teaspoons baking powder
¼ teaspoon salt
1 cup fresh blueberries

Preheat oven to 400 degrees F. Combine coconut milk, egg, honey, vanilla in a bowl and mix thoroughly. In a separate bowl mix together flour, coconut, baking powder, and salt. Add the dry ingredients to the wet, mixing just until moistened. Fold in the blueberries. Pour into muffin cups which have been coated with non-stick cooking oil (page 7) or coconut oil and bake for 15 minutes. Makes one dozen muffins.

Raspberry Coconut Muffins
Follow the directions for making Blueberry Coconut Muffins, substituting raspberries for the blueberries.

Cherry Coconut Muffins
Follow the directions for making Blueberry Coconut Muffins, substituting tart cherries for the blueberries.

> Unless otherwise noted, the term "flour" used in the recipes of this book means whole wheat flour. If you like, you may use white flour in these recipes and still achieve good results.

134

CINNAMON NUT MUFFINS

½ cup coconut milk
1 egg
2 tablespoons honey
1 teaspoon almond extract
½ cup flour
1 teaspoon baking powder
½ teaspoon cinnamon
¼ teaspoon salt
¼ cup pecans
2 tablespoons grated coconut

Preheat oven to 400 degrees F. Combine coconut milk, egg, honey, and almond extract in a bowl and mix thoroughly. In a separate bowl, mix together flour, baking powder, cinnamon, and salt. Add the dry ingredients to the wet, mixing just until moistened. Fold in pecans and coconut. Coat muffin cups with non-stick cooking oil (page 7) or coconut oil. Fill muffin cups. Bake for 15 minutes. Makes 6 muffins.

CORN BREAD MUFFINS

½ cup coconut milk
1 egg
2 tablespoons honey
1 teaspoon vanilla
¼ cup cornmeal
¼ cup flour
1 teaspoon baking powder
¼ teaspoon salt

Preheat oven to 400 degrees F. Combine coconut milk, egg, honey, and vanilla in a bowl and mix thoroughly. In a separate bowl, mix together cornmeal, flour, baking powder, and salt. Add the dry ingredients to the wet, mixing just until moistened. Coat muffin cups with non-stick cooking oil (page 7) or coconut oil. Fill muffin cups. Bake for 15 minutes. Makes 6 muffins.

Coconut Corn Bread Muffins
Make Corn Bread Muffins according to directions and add 2 tablespoons of grated coconut to batter.

WHOLE WHEAT COCONUT PANCAKES

1 cup whole wheat flour
1½ teaspoons baking powder
¼ teaspoon salt
¼ cup grated coconut
1 egg
1 tablespoon molasses
2 tablespoon coconut oil
1¼ cups lukewarm water

Mix flour, baking powder, salt, and coconut in bowl. In a separate bowl combine egg, molasses, 2 tablespoons coconut oil, and lukewarm water. Warm water is used to keep coconut oil from hardening. Honey can be substituted for the molasses if desired. Heat 2 teaspoons of coconut oil in a skillet. Mix the dry ingredients with the wet. Spoon batter onto hot skillet making pancakes about 2½ to 3 inches in diameter. Makes about 12 pancakes. Serve with your choice of syrup, fruit, or Coconut Sauce (page 56).

COCONUT MILK PANCAKES

1 cup flour
1 teaspoon baking powder
¼ teaspoon salt
1 egg
1½ cups coconut milk
1 teaspoon vanilla

Mix flour, baking powder, and salt in a bowl. In a separate bowl, mix together egg, coconut milk, and vanilla. Stir the dry ingredients into the wet. Heat 2 teaspoons of coconut oil in a skillet. Spoon batter onto hot skillet, making pancakes about 2½ to 3 inches in diameter. This recipe makes about 8 pancakes. For thinner pancakes add, a little water.

The non-stick cooking oil mentioned in this and other chapters is absolutely the best oil to use for baking. Foods do not stick to pans and clean up is quick and easy. See page 7 for the recipe for this remarkable oil.

ORANGE COCONUT PANCAKES

1 cup flour
1 teaspoon baking powder
¼ teaspoon salt
1 egg
¾ cup coconut milk
6 tablespoons orange juice concentrate, no water added

Mix flour, baking powder, and salt in a bowl. In a separate bowl, combine egg, coconut milk, and orange juice concentrate. Stir the dry ingredients into the wet. Heat 2 teaspoons of coconut oil in a skillet. Spoon batter onto hot skillet, making pancakes about 3 inches in diameter. Cook until puffed and dry around edges. Turn and cook other side. Serve with syrup or your favorite topping.

Fruity Coconut Pancakes
Make Orange Coconut Pancakes as directed but substitute any variety of frozen fruit juice concentrates for the orange juice.

COCONUTTY PANCAKES

¾ cup flour
½ cup shredded coconut
⅓ cup nuts
1 teaspoon baking powder
¼ teaspoon salt
2 eggs
¾ cup coconut milk
½ cup crushed pineapple

Mix together flour, coconut, nuts, baking powder, and salt in a bowl. In a separate bowl, combine eggs, coconut milk, and pineapple. Stir the dry ingredients into the wet. Heat 2 teaspoons of coconut oil in a skillet. Spoon batter onto hot skillet, making pancakes about 3 inches in diameter. Cook until puffed and dry around edges. Turn and cook other side. Serve with syrup or your favorite topping. Makes about 16 pancakes.

COCONUT BANANA PANCAKES

1 cup coconut milk
2 eggs
½ teaspoon almond extract
1 cup flour
½ cup grated coconut
1 tablespoon sugar
2 teaspoons baking powder
½ teaspoon salt
1 banana, sliced and quartered

In a medium bowl beat together coconut milk, eggs, and almond extract. In a separate bowl, mix flour, grated coconut, sugar, baking powder, and salt. Combine the wet and dry ingredients, mixing just until moistened. Cut banana into several slices and then cut each slice into quarters. Fold banana pieces into batter. For thinner pancakes add more coconut milk. Heat 2 teaspoons of coconut oil in a skillet. Drop batter onto hot skillet. Cook until small bubbles appear. Flip and cook other side until done. Top with Coconut Sauce (page 56) or syrup.

BAKED BLUEBERRY PANCAKE

2 tablespoons butter
3 eggs
1 can (14 ounces) coconut milk
¾ cup flour
2 tablespoons sugar
½ teaspoon salt
½ teaspoon cinnamon
1 cup blueberries

Preheat oven to 425 degrees F. Put butter into 10-inch pie plate and melt in the oven. Be careful not to burn the butter. While butter is melting, beat eggs, coconut milk, flour, sugar, and salt until smooth. Pour into hot pie plate. Bake for 20 minutes. Remove from oven and sprinkle top with cinnamon and blueberries. Bake 10 to 15 minutes longer or until knife inserted in center comes out clean and pancake is browned and puffed. Serve hot. If a sweeter pancake is desired, top with a little honey or whipped cream.

138

Baked Peach Pancake

Make recipe according to directions, substituting 1 to 2 cups of sliced peaches for the blueberries.

Reduced Sugar Baked Blueberry Pancake

Make recipe according to directions but omit the sugar and add a dash or two of stevia. Taste batter for desired sweetness before cooking.

CREPES

1 cup flour
1 teaspoon sugar
½ teaspoon baking powder
¼ teaspoon salt
2 eggs
1 can (14 ounces) coconut milk
2 tablespoons coconut oil, melted
1 teaspoon vanilla

Mix together flour, sugar, baking powder, and salt. Stir in eggs, coconut milk, coconut oil, and vanilla and beat until smooth. Heat at medium temperature 2 teaspoons of coconut oil in a 6- to 8-inch skillet. Pour ¼ cup of the batter into skillet; immediately rotate skillet until a thin even layer of batter covers the bottom of the skillet. Cook until light golden brown and edges begin to pull away from surface of pan. Run pancake turner around edge to loosen, turn and cook other side. Stack crepes, placing waxed paper between each layer to prevent sticking. Keep covered. To serve, cover one side of crepes with your choice of chopped fruit, nuts, jelly, and/or whipped cream. Roll up and sprinkle with powdered sugar.

FRENCH TOAST

2 eggs
¼ cup coconut milk
1 teaspoon cinnamon
⅛ teaspoon salt
4 slices of bread

Beat eggs, coconut milk, cinnamon, and salt together until smooth. Dip bread in egg mixture until completely covered. Melt 2 teaspoons of coconut oil in a skillet at medium temperature. Cook bread until golden brown, about 5 minutes on each side. Serve topped with fresh fruit or syrup.

SCONES ♥

Coconut oil
1 cup flour
1 teaspoon baking powder
½ teaspoon salt
2 eggs
1 tablespoon honey
¼ cup water
1 teaspoon vanilla

Fill saucepan up to ¾ of an inch with coconut oil and place on medium heat or use a deep fryer. Heat oil to about 325 degrees F. Mix together flour, baking powder, and salt. In a separate bowl thoroughly mix eggs, honey, water, and vanilla. Add dry ingredients and mix just until moist. Do not over mix. Drop batter by the spoonful into hot oil. Cook until bottom side is lightly browned, then turn over. Each side should cook about a minute or so. Remove from oil and place on paper towel to drain. Serve with powdered sugar and cinnamon, honey, jam, or syrup. Makes about 1½ dozen.

GRANOLA ♥

6 cups old fashioned oats
2 teaspoons cinnamon
4 cups shredded or flaked coconut
2 cups slivered or sliced almonds
1 cup virgin coconut oil
1 cup honey
1 tablespoon vanilla or almond extract

In a large bowl mix together oats, cinnamon, coconut, and almonds. Heat oil and honey in a small saucepan over medium heat until hot; remove from heat and add vanilla. Stir honey mixture into oat mixture. Pour into large baking dish. Bake at 325 degrees F for 1 hour and 15 minutes or until golden brown. Stir occasionally while cooking for even browning. Cool. Add raisins or dried fruit if desired.

Reduced Sugar Granola
Make granola as directed but replace honey with 1 cup of rice syrup. Add raisins or dried fruit if more sweetening is desired.

COCONUT OATMEAL ♥

1¾ cup water
¼ teaspoon salt
½ cup grated coconut
1 cup old fashioned oats
⅛ teaspoon almond extract

Bring water and salt to a rolling boil. Add coconut and oats, reduce and simmer for 5 minutes. Remove from heat, stir in almond extract, cover and let sit for 4 minutes. Add sweetener of your choice and serve with any one of the following: milk, coconut milk, Sweetened Coconut Milk (page 22), Powerhouse Mango Milk (page 38), or any Fresh Fruit Flavored Milk (page 23). Makes two servings.

Fresh Fruit Coconut Oatmeal
Make Coconut Oatmeal as directed and add fresh fruit cut into bite-size pieces. Tastes good with peaches, nectarines, pineapple, mango, papaya, banana, strawberries, blueberries, kiwi, boysenberries, raspberries, or blackberries.

Reduced Sugar Coconut Oatmeal
Make Coconut Oatmeal as directed, add fruit of your choice, and stevia to taste.

COCONUT RICE

½ cup brown rice
1½ cups water
1 cup coconut milk
1 teaspoon vanilla

2 tablespoons sucanat or honey
¼ teaspoon salt
1 cup shredded coconut, toasted

In a saucepan, soak rice in water for 4 hours or overnight. Keep rice covered as it soaks. Heat rice and water to boiling. Reduce heat, cover, and gently simmer for 45 minutes or until water is absorbed. Remove from heat. Mix in coconut milk, vanilla, sucanat, and salt. Serve topped with toasted coconut.

Fruit Coconut Rice

As a variation of the above recipe, you can add fresh cut fruit to the rice just before serving. Mangos, peaches, and strawberries make good accompaniments, but almost any fruit will work.

INDIAN-STYLE COCONUT RICE

This is a mildly spicy rice dish, which makes and excellent breakfast.

½ cup brown rice
1½ cups water
½ cup grated or shredded coconut
2 tablespoons raisins
2 tablespoons sucanat or other sweetener
¼ teaspoon ground cardamom
1 teaspoon ground cinnamon
¼ teaspoon salt
1 cup coconut milk
2 to 3 tablespoons slivered almonds, toasted

In a saucepan, soak rice in water for 4 hours or overnight. Keep rice covered as it soaks. Heat rice and water to boiling. Add coconut, raisins, sucanat, cardamom, cinnamon, and salt. Reduce heat, cover, and gently simmer for 45 minutes or until water is absorbed. Mix in coconut milk. Remove from heat. Serve topped with toasted almonds.

Reduced Sugar Indian-Style Coconut Rice

Follow the directions for making Indian-Style Coconut Rice but eliminate the sucanat, increase raisins to ½ cup, and add stevia to taste. Fresh fruit may also be added.

COCONUT MILK BISCUITS ♥

1 egg
½ cup coconut milk
2 tablespoons coconut oil
1 ½ cups flour
1 ½ teaspoons baking powder
½ teaspoon salt

Preheat oven to 400 degrees F. Egg and coconut milk should be at room temperature and coconut oil melted, but not hot. Combine wet ingredients. In a separate bowl mix dry ingredients. Add the dry ingredients to the wet and mix just until moistened. Roll dough into 1½-inch balls and place on ungreased cookie sheet. Flour hands to keep dough from sticking. Flatten each ball so that dough is about ½-inch thick. Bake for 20 minutes. Makes 8 biscuits.

CHEESE BISCUITS ♥

1 cup flour
1 teaspoon baking powder
½ teaspoon salt
2 tablespoons coconut oil
½ cup Thick Cheddar Cheese Sauce (page 58)
1 egg
2 tablespoons onions, diced

Preheat oven to 400 degrees F. Mix flour, baking powder, and salt together. In a separate bowl blend together melted coconut oil with warm (not hot) Thick Cheddar Cheese Sauce, stir in the egg and onion; the mixture will be lumpy. Add the flour. Dough will be very soft at this stage. Shape into 1½-inch balls, roll in flour to coat, and place on ungreased baking dish. Bake for 12 to 15 minutes. Makes about 8 biscuits.

Double Cheese Biscuits
This recipe is for those who love cheese. Make Cheese Biscuits as directed and add ½ cup of shredded cheese to batter.

YORKSHIRE PUDDING ♥

This delicious bread pudding is traditionally eaten with roast beef and smothered in gravy. Ordinarily Yorkshire Pudding is made with milk; this version, however, uses coconut milk.

2 eggs
1 cup coconut milk
1 cup flour
½ teaspoon salt
¼ cup meat drippings or butter

Preheat oven to 400 degrees F. In a blender, mix eggs, coconut milk, flour, and salt at high speed for about 1 to 2 minutes, until mixture is bubbly. Coat the bottom of a 9x9x2-inch pan with meat drippings or melted butter. Pour the mixture into the pan and bake for 20 minutes. Serve hot with gravy.

HUSH PUPPIES

Coconut oil
¾ cup cornmeal
½ cup flour
1 teaspoon baking powder
¾ teaspoon salt
1 teaspoon onion powder
1 cup coconut milk
1 egg
¼ cup onion, finely chopped
¼ cup red bell pepper, finely chopped
¼ cup whole corn

Heat oil to about 325 degrees F. Mix cornmeal, flour, baking powder, salt, and onion powder. Stir in coconut milk and egg. Fold in onion, bell pepper, and corn. Form batter into 1-inch balls and roll in flour. Drop batter in hot oil. Fry until brown, about 3 minutes.

For all baked goods I highly recommend coating the cookware with coconut oil based non-stick cooking oil. Baked goods almost slide out of pans with little effort. See page 7 for recipe.

COCONUT BANANA BREAD
WITH LIME GLAZE

2 cups flour
½ cup grated coconut
2 teaspoons baking powder
1 cup sucanat or sugar
½ teaspoon salt
½ cup coconut oil
2 large eggs
1 ½ cups mashed ripe banana (about 3 bananas)
1 teaspoon vanilla
Lime Glaze (below)

Preheat oven to 350 degrees F. Combine flour, coconut, baking powder, sugar, and salt in a bowl. In a separate bowl, blend coconut oil and eggs; mix in mashed banana and vanilla. Combine wet and dry ingredients and mix just until moist. Pour batter into an 8½x4½-inch loaf pan coated with a thin layer of non-stick cooking oil (page 7) or butter. Bake for 55 to 60 minutes or until knife inserted in center comes out clean. Cool loaf in pan for 10 minutes on a wire rack. Remove from pan and let cool completely on wire rack. Yields one loaf.

Lime Glaze
½ cup powdered sugar
1 ½ tablespoons fresh lime or lemon juice

Blend powdered sugar and juice. Drizzle over warm bread.

Reduced Sugar Coconut Banana Bread
Make Coconut Banana Bread as directed but reduce the sugar to ⅓ cup and add ¼ teaspoon stevia. Omit the glaze.

HAWAIIAN BANANA BREAD

2 cups flour
½ cup grated coconut
2 teaspoons baking powder
1 cup sucanat or sugar

½ teaspoon salt
½ cup coconut oil
2 eggs
1 ripe banana, mashed
1 can (8 ounces) crushed pineapple with juice
¼ cup orange juice concentrate, no water added

Preheat oven to 350 degrees F. Combine flour, coconut, baking powder, sugar, and salt in a bowl. In a separate bowl, blend coconut oil and eggs; mix in mashed banana, pineapple, and orange juice concentrate. Combine wet and dry ingredients and mix just until moist. Pour batter into an 8½x4½-inch loaf pan coated with a thin layer of non-stick cooking oil (page 7) or butter. Bake for 55 to 60 minutes or until knife inserted in center comes out clean. Cool loaf in pan for 10 minutes on a wire rack. Remove from pan and let cool completely on wire rack. Yields one loaf.

Reduced Sugar Hawaiian Banana Bread
Make Hawaiian Banana Bread as directed but reduce sugar to ⅓ cup and add ¼ teaspoon stevia.

ORANGE COCONUT BANANA BREAD

1 ½ cups flour
½ cup grated coconut
⅓ cup walnuts, chopped
¾ teaspoon baking powder
¾ cup sucanat or sugar
½ teaspoon salt
¼ cup coconut milk
2 large eggs
1 ½ cups mashed ripe banana (about 3 bananas)
1 ½ tablespoons grated orange rind
¼ cup orange juice concentrate, no water added

Preheat oven to 350 degrees F. Combine flour, coconut, nuts, baking powder, sugar, and salt in a bowl. In a separate bowl, mix together coconut milk, eggs, bananas, orange rind, and orange juice concentrate. Combine wet and dry ingredients and mix just until moist. Pour batter into an 8½x4½-inch loaf pan coated with a layer of non-stick cooking oil (page 7) or butter. Bake for 55 to 60 minutes or until knife inserted in center comes out clean. Cool loaf in pan for 10 minutes on a wire rack. Remove from pan and let cool completely on wire rack. Yields one loaf.

Reduced Sugar Orange Coconut Banana Bread
Make Orange Coconut Banana Bread as directed but reduce the sugar to ⅓ cup and add ¼ teaspoon stevia.

PUMPKIN NUT BREAD

1 ¼ cups flour
½ cup grated coconut
½ cup chopped nuts
1 teaspoon baking powder
½ teaspoon baking soda
¾ cup sucanat or sugar
1 teaspoon cinnamon
½ teaspoon nutmeg
1 teaspoon salt
1 cup coconut milk
2 eggs
1 cup pumpkin

Preheat oven to 350 degrees F. Combine flour, coconut, nuts, baking powder, baking soda, sugar, cinnamon, nutmeg, and salt in a bowl. In a separate bowl, blend together coconut milk, eggs, and pumpkin, Combine wet and dry ingredients and mix just until moist. Pour batter into an 8½x4½-inch loaf pan coated with a layer of non-stick cooking oil (page 7) or butter. Bake for 60 to 65 minutes or until knife inserted in center comes out clean. Cool loaf in pan for 10 minutes on a wire rack. Remove from pan and let cool completely on wire rack. Yields one loaf.

Reduced Sugar Pumpkin Nut Bread
Make Pumpkin Nut Bread as directed but reduce the sugar to ⅓ cup and add ¼ teaspoon stevia.

CHAPTER 10

Cakes

COCONUT CAKE

1 cup coconut milk
1 cup sugar
½ teaspoon vanilla
¼ teaspoon almond extract
2 eggs
1 cup whole wheat flour
2 teaspoons baking powder
¼ teaspoon salt
Coconut Frosting (below)

Preheat oven to 350 degrees F. Coat an 11x7x2-inch baking dish with a thin layer of coconut oil and dust with flour. Stir together coconut milk, sugar, vanilla, almond extract, and eggs. In a separate bowl sift flour, baking powder, and salt. Stir dry ingredients into the wet. Put batter into baking pan which has been coated with non-stick cooking oil (page 7) or butter. Bake 25 minutes or until light golden brown and cake begins to pull away from the sides of the pan. Top with Coconut Frosting below.

Coconut Frosting
2 tablespoons coconut oil, melted
¼ cup coconut milk
2 cups powdered sugar
1 teaspoon vanilla
⅛ teaspoon salt
½ cup shredded coconut, toasted

Cream coconut oil, milk, powdered sugar, vanilla, and salt together. Spread on cake and sprinkle top with toasted coconut.

Unless otherwise noted, the term "flour" refers to whole wheat flour. All dried coconut used in these recipes is unsweetened and the coconut milk is unsweetened. The term "sugar" means any dry sweetener. "Honey" means any liquid sweetener. I highly recommend coating your cookware with coconut oil based non-stick cooking oil (see page 7) for baking.

GERMAN CHOCOLATE CAKE ♥

This cake is made with Dutch cocoa, which is very popular in Europe. Dutching is a process which neutralizes the natural acidity in cocoa powder, producing a chocolate with a more mellow flavor. Regular cocoa can be substituted for Dutch cocoa if you like. The recipe below makes a single layer sheet cake or two layers of a 9-inch layer cake.

⅔ cup butter
⅔ cup Dutch Processed cocoa
1 cup coconut milk
1¾ cup sugar
1 teaspoon vanilla
4 eggs, separated
2½ cups flour
2 teaspoons baking powder
½ teaspoon salt
⅛ teaspoon cream of tartar
Coconut Pecan Frosting (below)

Melt butter and cocoa in small saucepan. Stir until smooth, remove from heat, and let cool slightly. Stir in coconut milk, sugar, vanilla, and egg yolks. In a bowl mix together flour, baking powder, and salt. Stir dry ingredients into chocolate mixture. In a separate bowl, beat egg whites and cream of tartar with an electric beater until soft peaks form. Fold egg whites into batter. Pour batter into a 13x9x2-inch baking dish that has been coated with a thin layer of non-stick cooking oil (page 7) or butter. Bake at 350 degrees F for 35 to 40 minutes or until knife inserted into center comes out clean. If you want to make a layer cake, use 2 round 9-inch pans and cook for about 30 minutes. Remove from oven and let cool. Cover top of cake with Coconut Pecan Frosting.

Coconut Pecan Frosting

This recipe makes enough frosting to frost only the top of the cake. If you want to frost the sides as well, double the recipe.

½ cup coconut milk
2 teaspoons cornstarch
½ cup sugar
1 egg yolk*
¼ cup butter
½ teaspoon vanilla

¾ *cup flaked coconut*
½ *cup pecans, chopped*

Mix coconut milk, cornstarch, sugar, egg yolk, and butter in a saucepan. Cook over medium heat, stirring constantly, until mixture thickens, about 5 or 6 minutes. Remove from heat and add vanilla, coconut, and pecans.

*The frosting does not use the egg white. However, you can make use of it by combining it with the egg whites used in the batter recipe.

Reduced Sugar German Chocolate Cake
Make the German Chocolate Cake as directed but reduce sugar to ¾ to 1 cup, add 1 tablespoon flour and ¼ teaspoon stevia. Make the frosting as directed but reduce sugar to ¼ cup.

BANANA COCONUT CAKE

2⅓ *cups flour*
1⅔ *cups sugar*
1¼ *teaspoons baking powder*
1 *teaspoon baking soda*
1 *teaspoon salt*
1 *cup coconut oil*
2 *eggs*
1½ *cups mashed ripe bananas (2 bananas)*
2 *teaspoons lemon juice*
¾ *cup shredded coconut*

Preheat oven to 350 degrees F. Mix flour, sugar, baking powder, baking soda, and salt into large mixing bowl. Add coconut oil, eggs, mashed banana, and lemon juice, and mix until all flour is dampened. Beat vigorously 2 minutes. Fold in coconut. Put a thin layer of non-stick cooking oil (page 7) or butter in 13x9x2-inch pan. Add batter and bake for 35 minutes or until knife inserted in center comes out clean. Cool 10 minutes in pan.

Reduced Sugar Banana Coconut Cake
Make the Banana Coconut Cake as directed but reduce sugar to ¾ cup, add ⅛ teaspoon stevia, and reduce coconut oil to ½ cup.

APPLESAUCE CAKE

2½ cups flour
1½ teaspoons baking soda
1 teaspoon salt
1 teaspoon ground cinnamon
½ teaspoon ground nutmeg
¼ teaspoon ground allspice
2 eggs
½ cup coconut oil
2 cups sugar
1½ cups applesauce
½ cup chopped pecans

In a bowl combine flour, baking soda, salt and spices. Set aside. Blend eggs and coconut oil together. Add in sugar and applesauce. Stir in flour mixture. Fold in pecans. Coat a 13x9x2-inch pan with a thin layer of non-stick cooking oil (page 7) or butter. Pour batter into pan and bake at 350 degrees F for 40 minutes or until knife inserted in center comes out clean. Cool 10 minutes in pan.

Reduced Sugar Applesauce Cake
Follow the directions for making the Applesauce Cake but reduce sugar to 1 cup, add ⅛ teaspoon stevia, and reduce applesauce to 1 cup.

COCONUT CARROT CAKE

2 cups flour
2 teaspoons baking soda
2 teaspoons cinnamon
½ teaspoon nutmeg
3 eggs
1½ cups coconut oil
1½ cups sucanat or sugar
1 teaspoon vanilla
1 can (8 ounces) crushed pineapple
2 cups carrots, grated
1 cup pecans, chopped
1 cup grated coconut

Mix flour, baking soda, cinnamon, and nutmeg together and set aside. Beat together eggs and melted (but not hot) coconut oil; mix in sugar, vanilla, and pineapple. Combine dry and wet ingredients and add carrots, pecans, and coconut. Coat a 13x9x2-inch baking pan with a thin layer of non-stick cooking oil (page 7) or butter. Pour batter into pan and bake at 350 degrees F or 35-40 minutes or until knife inserted in the center comes out clean. Top with your favorite frosting.

Reduced Sugar Coconut Carrot Cake

Follow the directions for making the Coconut Carrot Cake but reduce sugar to ¾ cup, add ⅛ teaspoon stevia, and reduce coconut oil to 1 cup.

STREUSEL COCONUT CAKE ♥

2 cups flour
1½ cups sucanat or sugar
3 teaspoons baking powder
1 teaspoon salt
⅓ cup butter
1 cup coconut milk
4 eggs, slightly beaten
Streusel (below)

Preheat oven to 350 Degrees F. Mix flour, sugar, baking powder, and salt together. Add butter, coconut milk, and eggs and stir until well blended. Coat a 13x9x2-inch baking pan with a thin layer of non-stick cooking oil (page 7) or butter. Pour batter into pan. Cover the top with Streusel. Bake for 35 to 40 minutes or until knife inserted in center comes out clean.

Streusel

½ cup chopped pecans
½ cup flaked or shredded coconut
⅓ cup sucanat or brown sugar
¼ cup flour
1 teaspoon ground cinnamon
3 tablespoons butter, softened
Stir all ingredients together into a crumbly mixture.

Pineapple Coconut Cake

Make the Streusel Coconut Cake as directed but substitute ¼ cup frozen orange juice concentrate (thawed) for ¼ cup of coconut milk. Add to batter 1 can (8½ ounces) of crushed pineapple, drained.

Blueberry Coconut Cake

Add 1 cup of blueberries to batter and make as directed.

Apple Coconut Cake

Peel and thinly slice 2 medium tart apples. Add to the batter and make as directed.

Reduced Sugar Streusel Coconut Cake

Prepare the batter as directed but reduce the sugar to ¾ cup and add ¼ teaspoon stevia. Follow the directions for the Streusel, reducing the sugar to 1 tablespoon. Spread 1 cup or 1 can (8½ ounces) of crushed pineapple, well drained, over top.

SPONGE CAKE ♥

7 large eggs, separated
½ teaspoon cream of tartar
2 cups flour
1½ cups sugar
3 teaspoons baking powder
½ teaspoon salt
1¼ cups coconut milk
1 teaspoon vanilla
Lemon Glaze (below)

Beat egg whites and cream of tartar until stiff peaks form, about 3 minutes; set aside. In a large mixing bowl combine flour, sugar, baking powder, and salt. Add coconut milk, egg yolks, and vanilla and mix with an electric beater until very smooth. Gradually and gently fold batter into egg whites with a rubber spatula, blending well. Coat a 13x9x2-inch baking pan with a thin layer of non-stick cooking oil (page 7) or butter. Pour batter into pan and bake at 350 degrees for 35 minutes or until top springs back when lightly touched. Let cool on wire rack. Frost with Lemon Glaze.

If desired, this cake can be made using a 10-inch tube pan. Follow recipe as directed but increase cooking time to 55 to 60 minutes. When cake is removed from the oven, immediately invert it onto funnel and let hang until completely cool. To remove cake from pan, run knife around outer edge of pan as well as tube. Remove from pan and glaze.

Lemon Glaze

2 cups powdered sugar
1 teaspoon vanilla
2 tablespoons fresh lemon juice
1 tablespoon coconut milk, or more for spreading consistency
2 teaspoons grated lemon peel

Thoroughly blend all ingredients together and spread on cooled cake.

Reduced Sugar Sponge Cake

Make Sponge Cake as directed but reduce sugar to ¾ cup and add ⅛ teaspoon stevia. Serve with Reduced Sugar Coconut Whipped Cream (page 176).

COCONUT CREAM CAKE

This is a layer cake using the Sponge Cake recipe and a cream filling. Follow the directions for making the Sponge Cake batter (page 154). Bake in two greased 9-inch layer cake pans at 350 degrees F for 20 to 25 minutes until cakes shrink slightly from sides of pans and are springy to the touch. Cool upright in pans on wire racks 5 minutes, then invert on racks, turn right side up, and allow to cool completely. Fill and frost with one of the fillings below.

Basic Vanilla Cream Filling

Makes about 1 cup, enough to fill an 8 or 9-inch 2-layer cake

¾ cup coconut milk
2 tablespoons cornstarch
⅓ cup sugar
1 egg yolk, lightly beaten with ¼ cup coconut milk
1 teaspoon vanilla
½ teaspoon imitation coconut extract (optional)

Mix together coconut milk, cornstarch, and sugar in a small saucepan. Over medium heat, stir constantly until mixture boils and thickens, boil and stir ½ minute longer. Remove from heat, slowly beat half of the hot mixture into egg yolk, and gradually return all to pan, beating constantly. Mix in vanilla and coconut extract and cool to room temperature.

Coconut Cream Cake Filling

Make a double recipe of Basic Vanilla Cream Filling above; divide in half and mix ½ cup flaked or shredded coconut into one part. Put cake layers together with coconut filling. Spread remaining filling over top and sides of cake, then coat thickly with flaked coconut (about 1½ cups).

Chocolate Coconut Cream Filling

Prepare as directed but add ½ cup of semisweet chocolate chips along with vanilla; blend well. Top with ½ cup flaked or shredded coconut.

Citrus Cream Filling

Prepare as directed but omit vanilla and add ¼ teaspoon lemon or orange extract and 2 teaspoons finely grated lemon or orange rind. Mix in ½ cup flaked or shredded coconut.

STRAWBERRY SHORTCAKE

The shortcake in this recipe is actually a sponge cake. A muffin pan is used so they look like cupcakes. Even with whole wheat flour this recipe makes an incredibly light and tasty cake.

1 cup flour
½ tablespoon baking powder
½ teaspoon salt
2 eggs, separated
½ cup coconut milk
¼ cup honey
1 teaspoon vanilla
⅛ teaspoon cream of tartar
3 to 4 cups sliced strawberries
Coconut Whipped Cream (page 175)

Preheat oven to 400 degrees F. Combine four, baking powder, and salt in mixing bowl. In another bowl blend together egg yolks, coconut milk, honey, and vanilla. Beat egg whites and cream of tartar until soft peaks form. Stir dry ingredients in egg yolk mixture. Fold egg whites into batter just until blended,

156

do not over mix. Put a thin layer of non-stick cooking oil (page 7) or butter into muffin cups. Fill cups half full. Bake for 15 minutes. Makes 12 cupcakes. Cut cakes in half and top each half with fresh strawberries and Coconut Whipped Cream.

Ginger Peach Shortcake

Make the shortcakes as directed but add ¼ cup chopped crystallized ginger to the batter. Top with sliced peaches and Coconut Whipped Cream.

Reduced Sugar Shortcakes

Make shortcakes as directed but reduce honey to 2 tablespoons and add a dash of stevia. Use Reduced Sugar Coconut Whipped Cream (page 176) with fresh strawberries for topping.

CINNAMON APPLE COCONUT CAKE

2 ½ cups flour
1 ¾ cups sucanat or sugar
2 teaspoons baking soda
1 teaspoon salt
1 cup coconut oil
4 eggs, slightly beaten
2 teaspoons vanilla
2 teaspoons cinnamon
3 cups tart apples, peeled and chopped
2 cups pecans, chopped
½ cup grated or shredded coconut
Coconut Whipped Cream (page 175)

Combine flour, sugar, baking soda, and salt. Mix in melted (not hot) coconut oil, eggs, and vanilla. Batter will be stiff. In a separate bowl, mix cinnamon, apples, pecans, and coconut together and fold into batter. Coat a 13x9x2-inch baking pan with a thin layer of non-stick cooking oil (page 7) or butter. Pour batter into pan and bake at 350 degrees F for 40 to 45 minutes or until knife inserted into center comes out clean. Cool in pan for 10 minutes. Serve topped with Coconut Whipped Cream.

Reduced Sugar Cinnamon Apple Coconut Cake

Follow the directions above but reduce sugar to ½ cup and add ⅛ teaspoon stevia.

CHAPTER 11

Cookies

COCONUT MACAROONS

2 egg whites
Dash of salt
½ teaspoon vanilla
⅔ cup sugar
1 cup shredded coconut

Beat egg whites with salt and vanilla until soft peaks form. Gradually add sugar, beating until stiff. Fold in coconut. Coat a cookie sheet with a thin layer of non-stick cooking oil (page 7) or a generous amount of butter. Drop batter by the rounded teaspoon onto the cookie sheet. Bake at 325 degrees F for 20 minutes. Makes about 1½ dozen.

Pecan Macaroons
Follow the directions for making Coconut Macaroons reducing coconut to ¾ cup and adding ½ cup of chopped pecans.

Coconut Almond Macaroons
Follow the directions for making Coconut Macaroons but substitute ½ teaspoon almond extract for the vanilla. Reduce coconut to ¾ cup and add ½ cup slivered almonds.

Chocolate Macaroons
Follow the directions for making Coconut Macaroons but add 1 tablespoon of milk chocolate chips.

Pineapple Macaroons
Put ½ cup of crushed or chopped pineapple on a paper towel and pat out excess moisture. Follow the directions for making Coconut Macaroons, adding the pineapple to the mixture.

Unless otherwise noted, the term "flour" refers to whole wheat flour. All dried coconut used in these recipes is unsweetened. The term "sugar" means any dry sweetener. "Honey" means any wet sweetener. Reduced sugar recipes are included for those who want to limit their sugar intake. To keep cookies from sticking I highly recommend using the non-stick cooking oil described on page 7.

Reduced Sugar Macaroons

Make the Coconut Macaroons according to recipe but reduce the sugar to ¼ cup and add a dash or two of stevia. You can make any of the Macaroon variations described above using this procedure.

COCONUT KISSES

These cookies are similar to Macaroons but with a crispy crunch.

3 egg whites
½ teaspoon vanilla
¾ cup sugar
Dash of salt
2 cups crisp rice cereal
1 cup shredded or grated coconut
½ cup chopped almonds or macadamia nuts

Beat egg whites, vanilla, and salt until soft peaks form. Gradually add sugar, beating until stiff peaks form. Fold in cereal, coconut, and nuts. Coat a cookie sheet with a thin layer of non-stick cooking oil (page 7) or a generous amount of butter. Drop batter from teaspoon onto cookie sheet. Bake at 350 degrees F for 15 to 18 minutes. Remove cookies from pan immediately. If they stick to pan, reheat in oven to soften.

Reduced Sugar Coconut Kisses

Make Coconut Kisses as directed but reduce sugar to ¼ cup and add a dash or two of stevia.

NUTTY CHOCOLATE CHIP ♥

½ cup butter
½ cup sucanat or brown sugar
1 egg
1 teaspoon vanilla
1¼ cups flour
½ cup grated coconut
½ teaspoon salt
½ teaspoon baking powder

½ cup semisweet chocolate chips
½ cup chopped pecans

Combine butter, sugar, egg, and vanilla. Mix together flour, coconut, salt, and baking powder; blend into egg mixture. Add chocolate chips and pecans. Drop from teaspoon 2 inches apart on ungreased cookie sheet. Bake at 375 degrees F for 10 to 12 minutes. Remove from baking sheet immediately. Makes about 3 dozen.

Reduced Sugar Nutty Chocolate Chip
Make the Nutty Chocolate Chip recipe according to directions but reduce sugar to ¼ cup and add a dash or two of stevia.

COCONUT MERINGUE BARS

¾ cup butter
3 eggs, separated
½ cup sucanat or brown sugar
½ teaspoon vanilla
2 cups flour
1 teaspoon baking powder
1 teaspoon baking soda
¼ teaspoon salt
1 cup semisweet chocolate chips
1 cup flaked coconut
1 cup coarsely chopped nuts
½ cup sugar
½ cup grated coconut

Preheat oven to 350 degrees F. Blend together butter, egg yolks, ½ cup sucanat or brown sugar, and vanilla and set aside. In a separate bowl mix flour, baking powder, baking soda, and salt. Mix wet and dry mixtures together. Fold in chocolate chips, coconut, and nuts. Coat a 13x9x2-inch pan with a thin layer of non-stick cooking oil (page 7) or a generous amount of butter. Press batter into the pan.

Beat egg whites until foamy. Continue beating while adding ½ cup sugar, 1 tablespoon at a time; beat until stiff peaks form. Beat in grated coconut. Spread over mixture in pan. Bake 35 to 40 minutes. Cool; cut into bars.

Reduced Sugar Coconut Meringue Bars

Make Coconut Meringue Bars as directed but reduce sugar to ¼ cup and add a dash or two of stevia. Reduce sugar in the meringue to ¼ cup.

CARROT COCONUT COOKIES

1 cup mashed cooked carrots
¾ cup sugar
1 cup butter or coconut oil
2 eggs
2 cups flour
2 teaspoons baking powder
½ teaspoon salt
¾ cup shredded or flaked coconut
Orange Butter Frosting (see below)

Preheat oven to 400 degrees F. Mix carrots, sugar, coconut oil, and eggs. Stir in flour, baking powder, and salt. Stir in coconut. Drop dough by the teaspoonful about 2 inches apart onto ungreased cookie sheet. Bake for 8 minutes or until almost no indentation remains when touched. Immediately remove from cookie sheet; cool and frost with Orange Butter Frosting.

Orange Butter Frosting

1½ cups powdered sugar
¼ cup butter
2 tablespoons orange juice
1 tablespoon grated orange peel

Mix powdered sugar and butter. Stir in orange juice; beat until frosting is smooth.

Reduced Sugar Carrot Coconut Cookies

Make the batter for the Carrot Coconut Cookies as directed but reduce sugar to ¼ cup and add ⅛ teaspoon stevia. Reduce the powdered sugar in the Orange Butter Frosting to 1 cup, add a dash of stevia, and reduce butter to 3 tablespoons.

COCONUT OATMEAL COOKIES

1 cup brown sugar
½ cup butter or coconut oil
1 egg
½ teaspoon vanilla
1 cup flour
1 cup quick-cooking or old fashioned oats
½ cup flaked coconut
½ teaspoon baking soda
¼ teaspoon salt
1½ teaspoons cinnamon
½ teaspoon nutmeg
½ cup chopped walnuts

Mix together sugar, butter, egg, and vanilla. In a separate bowl combine flour, oats, coconut, baking soda, salt, cinnamon, and nutmeg; stir into wet mixture. Fold in nuts. Drop on ungreased cookie sheet. Bake at 375 degrees F for 10 minutes.

Reduced Sugar Coconut Oatmeal Cookies
Make Coconut Oatmeal Cookies as described above but reduce sugar to ½ cup, and add a dash or two of stevia. If desired, you can leave out the stevia and add ½ cup raisins.

CHOCOLATE COCONUT OATMEAL COOKIES

1 cup brown sugar
½ cup butter
1 egg
½ teaspoon vanilla
1 cup flour
1 cup quick-cooking or old fashion oats
½ cup flaked coconut
½ teaspoon baking soda
¼ teaspoon salt
½ cup chopped pecans
½ cup semisweet chocolate chips

Combine sugar, butter, egg, and vanilla. In a separate bowl, mix flour, oats, coconut, baking soda, and salt; stir into wet mixture. Fold in nuts and chocolate chips. Drop on ungreased cookie sheet. Bake at 375 degrees F for 10 minutes.

Reduced Sugar Chocolate Coconut Oatmeal Cookies

Make Coconut Oatmeal Cookies as described above but reduce sugar to ½ cup and add ⅛ teaspoon stevia.

PECAN COCONUT BARS

Bottom Layer
1 cup brown sugar
1 cup butter
2 eggs
1 teaspoon vanilla
2 cups flour
¼ teaspoon salt
Top Layer
½ cup sucanat or brown sugar
2 tablespoons flour
¼ cup butter or coconut oil, softened
½ cup pecans
½ cup flaked coconut

Preheat oven to 350 degrees F. For the bottom layer, mix together brown sugar, butter, eggs, and vanilla. Stir in flour and salt. Coat a 13x9x2-inch pan with a thin layer of non-stick cooking oil (page 7) or a generous amount of butter. With your hands, press batter into the pan. To prevent dough from sticking to your hands, keep them dry by dusting them in flour. Set aside.

For the top layer, mix remaining ingredients and spread over bottom layer. Bake for 35 to 40 minutes or until knife inserted in center comes out clean. Cool, cut into bars.

Reduced Sugar Pecan Coconut Bars

Make bottom layer of above recipe as directed except reduce brown sugar to ½ cup and butter to ¾ cup. Make the top layer as directed but reduce sugar to ¼ cup.

164

CHOCOLATE COCONUT BARS ♥

1 cup brown sugar
1 cup butter
2 eggs
1 teaspoon vanilla
2 cups flour
¼ teaspoon salt
⅔ cup milk chocolate chips
½ cup almonds, chopped and toasted
1 cup flaked coconut, toasted

Preheat oven to 350 degrees F. Mix together brown sugar, butter, eggs, and vanilla. Stir in flour and salt; add toasted almonds. Coat a 13x9x2-inch pan with a thin layer of non-stick cooking oil (page 7) or a generous amount of butter. With your hands, press batter into the pan. To prevent dough from sticking to your hands, keep them dry by dusting them in flour. Bake for 25 to 30 minutes or until very light brown. Remove from oven; sprinkle chocolate chips over the hot crust. Let stand until chips soften and spread evenly over the crust. Sprinkle top with toasted coconut.

Reduced Sugar Chocolate Coconut Bars
Make Chocolate Coconut Bars as directed but reduce sugar to ½ cup and add ⅛ teaspoon stevia. Sprinkle toasted coconut on top as directed.

COCONUT SUGAR COOKIES

3 cups flour
1½ teaspoons baking powder
1 teaspoon salt
1¼ cups coconut oil
1½ cups sugar
1½ teaspoons almond extract
3 eggs
1½ cups grated coconut

Preheat oven to 375 degrees F. Mix flour, baking powder, and salt and set aside. Combine coconut oil, sugar, and almond extract. Add eggs, 1 at a time, beating well after each addition. Add coconut and slowly mix into dry ingredients until just blended. If your kitchen is very hot, wrap dough in wax paper and chill about 1 hour so it will roll more easily. Roll ¼ of dough at a time on a lightly floured board to about ¼-inch thickness. Use cookie cutter or top of drinking glass to cut cookies. Lightly coat cookie sheet with `non-stick cooking oil` (`page 7`) or butter. Using a pancake turner, transfer cookie dough to cookie sheet, spacing cookies 2 inches apart. Bake for 12-15 minutes until pale tan. Transfer to wire racks to cool.

Reduced Sugar Coconut Sugar Cookies
Make Coconut Sugar Cookies as directed but reduce sugar to ¾ cup and add ⅛ teaspoon stevia.

ALMOND COCONUT COOKIES

2 eggs, separated
1 cup butter
1½ cups sucanat or brown sugar
½ teaspoon almond extract
2½ cups flour
¾ cup almonds, chopped
1 teaspoon baking powder
2 teaspoons cream of tartar
¼ teaspoon salt
Shredded or flaked coconut

Separate the egg yolks from the whites. Mix the egg yolks with butter, sugar, and almond extract and set aside. In a separate bowl, mix together flour, almonds, baking powder, cream of tartar, and salt. Stir the wet and dry ingredients together. Roll dough into balls and dip into egg whites, then into coconut, and place on ungreased cookie sheet. Bake at 350 degrees F for 12 to 15 minutes or until coconut is lightly browned. Remove from baking sheet immediately and cool on wire rack.

Reduced Sugar Almond Coconut Cookies
Make above recipe according to directions but reduce sugar to ¾ cup and add ⅛ teaspoon stevia.

APRICOT COCONUT BARS ♥

1 cup brown sugar
1 cup butter or coconut oil
2 eggs
1 teaspoon vanilla
2 cups flour
¼ teaspoon salt
1 cup apricot jam or preserves
½ cup walnuts, chopped
½ cup flaked coconut

Mix together brown sugar, butter, eggs, and vanilla. Stir in flour and salt. Apply a thin layer of non-stick cooking oil (page 7) or butter to a 13x9x2-inch pan. With your hands, press dough into pan. To prevent dough from sticking to your hands, keep them dry by dusting them in flour. Spread an even layer of apricot jam over the batter. Cover the jam with walnuts and coconut. Bake at 350 degrees F for 35 to 40 minutes or until a knife inserted in the center comes out clean. Cool and cut into bars.

Reduced Sugar Apricot Coconut Bars
Make the Apricot Coconut Bars according to recipe except reduce sugar to ½ cup and add ⅛ teaspoon stevia. Use "Low Sugar" apricot preserves. Smucker's makes an apricot preserve with 50 percent less sugar than what is usually used.

HAYSTACKS

These cookies look much like miniature stacks of hay and taste very similar to coconut macaroons.

¼ cup butter or coconut oil
1 cup sugar
4 eggs
½ teaspoon vanilla
¼ teaspoon almond extract
¼ cup flour
4 cups grated or flaked coconut

Mix together butter, sugar, eggs, vanilla, and almond extract. Stir in flour and coconut. Put a layer of non-stick cooking oil (page 7) or butter on a cookie sheet. Drop spoon-size mounds 1-inch apart on cookie sheet. Bake at 375 degrees F for 18 to 20 minutes or until golden brown. Remove from cookie sheet immediately and cool on wire rack.

Chocolate Haystacks

Make Haystacks according to directions but add ½ cup of milk chocolate chips to batter.

Butterscotch Haystacks

Make Haystacks according to directions but add ½ cup of butterscotch chips to batter.

Reduced Sugar Haystacks

Make Haystacks following directions above but reduce sugar to ½ cup and add ⅛ teaspoon of stevia.

COCONUT SESAME BALLS ♥

¼ cup sesame seeds
¼ cup sunflower seeds
¾ cup shredded coconut
3 tablespoons peanut butter*
2 tablespoons rice syrup**

Put sesame seeds and sunflower seeds in an oven safe pan. Put the coconut in a second pan. Heat oven to 350 degrees and bake seeds and coconut for about 8 to 12 minutes or until lightly toasted. Coconut cooks faster and will need to be taken out first. Blend peanut butter and rice syrup, add toasted sesame seeds, sunflower seeds, and coconut and mix together. Spoon mixture into bite-size balls and place on wax paper. Put into the refrigerator to harden.

*You may substitute tahini or almond butter for the peanut butter if you desire.

**You may substitute 1 tablespoon honey for the rice syrup in this recipe, but balls will be softer and a little more difficult to shape.

CHOCOLATE CRISPS ♥
This is one of those treats that should be reserved for those with a great deal of willpower. They're so unbelievably good that you can't eat *just* one.

1 cup chopped almonds, toasted
1 cup flaked coconut, toasted
2 cups milk chocolate chips

Toast almonds and coconut in oven at 350 degrees for about 8 to 10 minutes. Use 2 separate dishes because coconut toasts quicker. Melt chocolate chips in saucepan over low heat, stirring frequently. Don't overcook! Heat just until slightly melted. When chocolate is soft, remove from heat and stir in toasted almonds and coconut. Drop by tablespoon onto wax paper and cool. If kitchen is too warm, you may need to put them into the refrigerator to set. Store in a cool place or refrigerator.

Chocolate Crispies
Make Chocolate Crisps as directed but replace almonds with 1 cup crisp rice cereal.

Peanut Butter Crispies
Make Chocolate Crispies above with crisp rice cereal and add ½ cup peanut butter.

Rocky Road Crisps
Make Chocolate Crisps as directed but substitute 1 cup of pecans for the almonds and add 1 cup of miniature marshmallows.

GRANOLA BARS

3½ cup oats
1 cup flaked coconut
1 cup raisins
1 cup nuts, chopped
⅔ cup butter*
½ cup sucanat or brown sugar
⅓ cup corn syrup or honey
½ teaspoon salt
1 egg, beaten
½ teaspoon vanilla

Mix first 8 ingredients together. Combine egg and vanilla and stir into mix. Coat a 13x9x2-inch baking dish with non-stick cooking oil (page 7) or butter. Press granola firmly into baking dish. Bake at 325 degrees for 40 minutes. Remove from oven and let cool completely. Cut into bars.

*You may substitute a mixture of ⅓ cup butter and ⅓ cup coconut oil if your desire.

Reduced Sugar Granola Bars

Make Granola Bars as directed but delete sucanat and corn syrup, add ½ cup rice syrup, and ⅛ teaspoon stevia.

CHOCOLATE GRANOLA BARS ♥

1 cup almonds, chopped and toasted
3½ cup oats
1 cup flaked coconut
½ cup semisweet chocolate chips
⅔ cup butter*
½ cup sucanat or brown sugar
⅓ cup corn syrup or honey
½ teaspoon salt
1 egg, beaten
½ teaspoon vanilla

Toast almonds in oven at 350 degrees for 10 minutes. Mix almonds and next 7 ingredients together. Combine egg and vanilla and stir into oat mixture. Coat a 13x9x2-inch baking dish with non-stick cooking oil (page 7) or butter. Press granola firmly into baking dish. Bake at 325 degrees for 40 minutes. Remove from oven and let cool completely. Cut into bars.

*You may substitute a mixture of ⅓ cup butter and ⅓ cup coconut oil if you desire.

COCONUT BUTTER COOKIES

3 cups flour
1½ cups grated coconut
1½ teaspoons baking powder
1 teaspoon salt
1 cup butter
1½ cups sugar
2 teaspoons vanilla extract
3 eggs

Preheat oven to 375 degrees F. Mix flour, grated coconut, baking powder, and salt and set aside. Blend butter, sugar, vanilla extract, and eggs. Mix together wet and dry ingredients. Form dough into balls 1½-inches in diameter. Place on ungreased cookie sheet 2 inches apart. Bake for 12 to 15 minutes until pale tan. Transfer to wire racks to cool. Makes about 3 dozen cookies.

CHAPTER 12

Pies

PASTRY

COCONUT OIL PASTRY

Using coconut oil to make pie crust produces excellent results. The following recipes are for a single-crust and a double-crust 8-, 9-, or 10-inch pie. These recipes work equally well with either whole wheat or white flour. The only difference is that whole wheat crust often needs 1 or 2 tablespoons more water than white flour. The secret to making good piecrusts using coconut oil is to chill the oil before cutting it into the flour. The kitchen should be 72 degrees or cooler for best results. If you have a food processor, cutting the oil into the flour is quick and simple.

Single-Crust

1¼ cups flour
½ teaspoon salt
⅓ cup coconut oil, chilled
4 to 5 tablespoons ice water (5 to 6 for whole wheat)

Double-Crust

2 cups flour
1 teaspoon salt
⅔ cup coconut oil, chilled
5 to 7 tablespoons ice water (7 to 8 for whole wheat)

Mix flour and salt together, cut hardened coconut oil into flour in a food processor until pieces are between the size of small peas and coarse cornmeal. If you don't have a food processor, you can mix it by hand with a pastry blender or fork and knife. Gradually add ice water, a tablespoon at a time, until moistened and pastry begins to stick together and not to the container.

Put a strip of wax paper on a flat surface. Tape edges of paper down so it doesn't move. Lightly flour surface of wax paper. Gather pastry into a ball; flatten out on wax paper. Lightly flour rolling pin and flatten pastry until about ⅛-inch thick. (For two-crust pie, divide pastry into halves and shape each individually.) Add more flour to rolling pin as needed to prevent pastry from sticking.

Lift wax paper from flat surface with one hand underneath the paper and one on pastry, and gently turn upside down into pie plate (or fold half of pastry over pin and ease into pan). Remove wax paper and shape crust into plate, pressing firmly against bottom and sides. Seal any cracks or holes by pressing dampened scraps of pastry on top. Trim overhanging edge of pastry and flute as desired. Fill and bake as directed in each recipe.

Baked Single-Crust Pie Shell. Prick bottom and side thoroughly with fork to avoid shrinkage and distortion of shell during baking. Bake at 450 degrees F or 10 to 12 minutes.

Double-Crust Pie. Leave 1-inch trim of top pastry beyond edge of plate. Fold and roll rim of top pastry under edge of bottom pastry, then press together to seal. Edge can be fluted in any manner you wish for an attractive finish. Cut several slits in the top crust to allow steam to escape. Bake as directed in recipe.

Tart Pastry Shells. Tarts are basically miniature pies. Each pie is an individual serving. Prepare pastry as you would for a full size pie. If you want to make 4 double-crust tart shells, use the Double-Crust recipe. Divide the pasty into 8 balls. Roll them out into 5- to 6-inch circles and place bottom crust into 4 tart pans or custard cups. Fill tarts with filling and cover with a top crust. Bake as directed in recipe. You can use tart shells to make any of the pie recipes that follow.

COCONUT PASTRY SHELL

This pastry shell contains grated coconut.

1 cup flour
½ cup grated coconut
¼ teaspoon salt
½ cup coconut oil, chilled
3 to 4 tablespoons ice water

Mix flour and grated coconut together. Follow the recipe above for making the Coconut Oil Pastry Shell using the flour/coconut mixture. Makes a single crust.

> All dried coconut used in these recipes is unsweetened and the coconut milk is unsweetened.

174

TOPPINGS

MERINGUE

3 egg whites
½ teaspoon vanilla
¼ teaspoon cream of tartar
¼ cup sugar

Beat egg whites, vanilla, and cream of tartar until soft peaks form. Gradually add sugar, beating until stiff and sugar is dissolved. Spread meringue over hot pie filling, spreading all the way to the edge of the pastry (this helps prevent the meringue from shrinking). Bake at 350 degrees F for 12 to 15 minutes, or until meringue is golden brown. Cool.

Reduced Sugar Meringue

Make meringue as directed but reduce sugar to 2 tablespoons and add a dash of powdered stevia extract. Be careful not to use too much stevia. A little can go a long way and too much will give the meringue a bitter aftertaste. Use just a tiny bit and gradually add more if you want the meringue to be sweeter.

COCONUT WHIPPED CREAM ♥

This recipe uses a mixture of heavy whipping cream and coconut cream.

½ cup plus 2 tablespoons heavy cream
½ teaspoon imitation coconut extract or 1 teaspoon vanilla
3 tablespoons powdered sugar
½ cup coconut cream*

Combine heavy cream and coconut extract into a bowl. Whip the cream until soft peaks form. Add sugar and beat until stiff peaks form. Whip in coconut cream. This may cause it to lose some of its volume depending on the thickness of the coconut cream but that's okay. Chill and serve cold. Makes about 1½ cups.

*If you don't have coconut cream, you can use coconut milk. Use the creamiest portion of the milk. The thickness of the coconut cream you use will determine the thickness of the whipped cream you end up with. The cream in many brands of coconut milk naturally separates out and rises to the top. When you open a can of coconut milk, you can scoop out the cream. Be careful not to shake the can before opening. Refrigerating coconut milk several days before opening causes more of the cream to separate and rise to the top.

Almond Whipped Cream
Prepare Coconut Whipped Cream as directed but replace coconut extract with ½ teaspoon of almond extract.

Peppermint Whipped Cream
Prepare Coconut Whipped Cream as directed but replace coconut extract with ½ teaspoon of peppermint extract.

Maple Whipped Cream
Prepare Coconut Whipped Cream as directed but replace coconut extract with ¼ teaspoon maple flavoring.

Chocolate Whipped Cream
Prepare Coconut Whipped Cream as directed but add 3 tablespoons powdered cocoa, increase powdered sugar to 6 tablespoons, and use ½ teaspoon vanilla extract and ½ teaspoon imitation coconut extract. Makes about 2½ cups.

Reduced Sugar Coconut Whipped Cream
Prepare Coconut Whipped Cream as directed but reduce powdered sugar to 1 tablespoon and add a pinch or two of powdered stevia extract. Be careful not to use too much stevia. A little can go a long way. Use just a tiny bit, taste the whipped cream, and gradually add more if you want it sweeter.

PIES

SUPER DELICIOUS COCONUT PIE ♥
This is a delicious and easy-to-make pie.

3 eggs, beaten
2 tablespoons flour
1 ½ cup sugar
½ cup butter, melted

4 teaspoons lemon juice
1 teaspoon vanilla
1⅓ cup grated coconut
Dash of salt
1 9-inch unbaked pastry shell
Coconut Whipped Cream (page 175)

Preheat oven to 350 degrees F. Combine all ingredients except whipped cream and mix well. Pour into unbaked pastry shell and bake for 40 to 45 minutes, until top forms a golden crust and knife inserted in center comes out clean. Cool and top with Coconut Whipped Cream.

Reduced Sugar Super Delicious Coconut Pie

Make the Super Delicious Coconut Pie as directed but reduce sugar to ¾ cup, add up to ⅛ teaspoon stevia, and reduce lemon juice to 3 teaspoons. May be served with or without whipped cream; it's good either way.

FROZEN COCONUT PIE ♥

½ cup sugar
¾ cup coconut milk
1¼ cup flaked coconut
½ teaspoon almond extract
Coconut Whipped Cream (page 175)
1 9-inch baked pastry shell

Combine sugar, coconut milk, coconut, and almond extract. Let mixture sit for about 5 minutes to allow sugar to dissolve. Fold in 1½ cups of Coconut Whipped Cream. Pour into baked pastry shell and freeze for at least 4 hours. Thaw for 15 minutes before serving.

Frozen Chocolate Coconut Pie

Make Frozen Coconut Pie as directed but reduce coconut milk to ½ cup and flaked coconut to 1 cup. Replace Coconut Whipped Cream with 2½ cups (1 recipe) Chocolate Coconut Whipped Cream (page 176).

VANILLA CREAM PIE

¾ cup sugar
3 tablespoons cornstarch
¼ teaspoon salt
1 can (14 ounces) coconut milk
3 slightly beaten egg yolks
2 tablespoons butter
1 tablespoon vanilla
1 9-inch baked pastry shell
Meringue (3 egg whites, page 175)

In saucepan, combine sugar, cornstarch, and salt; stir in coconut milk. Cook and stir over medium heat until bubbly. Cook and stir 2 minutes. Remove from heat. Slowly stir at least ½ cup of hot mixture into yolks and immediately return to hot mixture; cook 4 minutes, stirring constantly. Remove from heat. Add butter and vanilla. Pour into cooled *baked* pastry shell. Spread meringue on top of pie and bake at 350 degrees F for 12 to 15 minutes, until meringue is a golden brown. Cool and store in refrigerator. Serve chilled.

Chocolate Cream Pie
Prepare Vanilla Cream Pie, increasing sugar to 1 cup. Add two 1-ounce squares of unsweetened chocolate with the coconut milk. Top with meringue and bake as directed.

Banana Cream Pie
Slice 3 bananas and put into cooled baked 9-inch pastry shell. Add Vanilla Cream or Chocolate Cream Pie filling. Top with meringue and bake as directed.

Coconut Cream Pie
Add 1 cup of grated coconut to Vanilla Cream Pie filling. Cover with meringue and sprinkle the top with ⅓ cup shredded or flaked coconut. Bake as directed.

Peppermint Cream Pie
Add 1 teaspoon of peppermint extract to Vanilla Cream Pie filling. Top with meringue or Peppermint Whipped Cream (page 176). Serve with crushed peppermint candy sprinkled on top.

Caramel Cream Pie
Replace granulated sugar with sucanat.

Reduced Sugar Cream Pies

Make pies as directed but reduce sugar to ⅓ cup and add ⅛ teaspoon stevia. For reduced sugar Chocolate Cream Pie use ¾ cup sugar and enough stevia to suit your taste.

LEMON CHIFFON PIE

1 envelope unflavored gelatin
1 cup sugar
½ teaspoon salt
4 egg yolks
⅓ cup lemon juice
⅓ cup water
⅔ cup coconut milk
½ teaspoon grated lemon peel
4 egg whites
⅛ teaspoon cream of tartar
1 9-inch baked pastry shell, cooled

In saucepan, combine gelatin, ½ cup of the sugar, and salt. In bowl mix together egg yolks, lemon juice, ⅓ cup water, and ⅔ cup coconut milk. Stir into gelatin mixture. Cook over medium heat, stirring constantly until mixture comes to a boil and gelatin dissolves. Remove from heat and stir in peel. Chill, stirring occasionally, until partially set but still pourable (about 45 minutes). Combine egg whites and cream of tartar. With an electric beater, beat egg whites until soft peaks form. Gradually add remaining sugar, beating until stiff peaks form. Fold in partially set gelatin mixture. Put into cooled baked pastry shell. Chill until firm, about 3 to 5 hours.

STRAWBERRY CHIFFON PIE ♥

2 cups fresh strawberries, sliced
½ cup sugar
⅓ cup water
1 envelopelope (¼ ounce) unflavored gelatin
⅔ cup coconut milk
1 tablespoon lemon juice

Dash of salt
2 egg whites
⅛ teaspoon cream of tartar
1 9-inch baked pastry shell, cooled

Crush strawberries; add ¼ cup of the sugar; let stand for 30 minutes. In the meantime bring water to a boil, remove from heat, and let sit for 1 minute. Stir in gelatin and allow to cool about 5 minutes. Add gelatin, coconut milk, lemon juice, and dash of salt to the strawberry mix. Chill, stirring occasionally, until partially set but still pourable (about 45 minutes). In a mixing bowl add egg whites and cream of tartar. Beat egg whites to soft peaks; gradually add the remaining ¼ cup sugar, beating until stiff peaks form. Fold in strawberry mixture. Fill cooled baked pastry shell. Chill until firm, about 3 to 5 hours.

Reduced Sugar Strawberry Chiffon Pie
Make pie as directed but increase strawberries to 3 cups, reduce lemon juice to 2 teaspoons, reduce sugar in the gelatin mixture to 1 tablespoon, add ⅛ teaspoon stevia, and reduce sugar in the egg whites to 2 tablespoons. You may adjust the amount of sugar and stevia you use to suit your taste.

CHOCOLATE CHIFFON PIE

1 envelope (¼ ounce) unflavored gelatin
¼ cup water
3 egg yolks
¼ teaspoon salt
1 teaspoon vanilla
¾ cup sugar
2 1-ounce squares unsweetened chocolate
½ cup coconut milk
3 egg whites
⅛ teaspoon cream of tartar
1 9-inch baked pastry shell, cooled

Soften gelatin in ¼ cup cold water. In mixing bowl, beat egg yolks together then gradually beat in salt, vanilla, and ½ cup of the sugar. In a saucepan combine chocolate and coconut milk; stir over low heat until melted; add softened gelatin and stir to dissolve. Mix egg yolk mixture into chocolate mixture; remove from heat. Chill, stirring occasionally, until mixture is partially set but still pourable (about 45 minutes). In a separate bowl, combine egg whites and cream of tartar. With an electric better, beat egg whites to soft peaks. Gradually add ¼ cup sugar, beating to stiff peaks. Add egg whites into chilled chocolate mixture; fold in just until blended. Fill baked pie shell. Chill until firm. Top with whipped cream.

BLACK BOTTOM CUSTARD PIE

Bottom Layer
1 can (14 ounces) coconut milk
4 beaten egg yolks
½ cup sugar
2 tablespoons cornstarch
1 teaspoon vanilla
1 6-ounce package (1 cup) semisweet chocolate chips
1 9-inch baked pastry shell

Top Layer
1 envelope unflavored gelatin
¼ cup water
½ teaspoon almond extract
4 egg whites
½ cup sugar
Sliced almonds, toasted

Mix coconut milk and egg yolks together, stir in ½ cup sugar and cornstarch. Cook and stir over medium heat until custard thickens. Remove from heat and add vanilla. Put 1 cup of hot custard in a separate bowl along with chocolate chips, stir until melted (you will have some custard left over to be used below). Pour into baked pastry shell and chill.

Meanwhile, soften gelatin by combining it with ¼ cup water and remaining *hot* custard. Stir until dissolved. Mix in almond extract. Chill until slightly thickened. Beat egg whites until soft peaks form; gradually add ½ cup sugar; beat again until stiff peaks form. Fold into chilled custard-gelatin mixture. Remove half filled pie from refrigerator and pour mixture on top of chocolate layer. Sprinkle top with lightly toasted sliced almonds. Chill until set.

COCONUT CUSTARD PIE

4 slightly beaten eggs
2 tablespoons flour
½ cup sugar
¼ teaspoon salt
1 tablespoon vanilla
1 can (14 ounces) coconut milk
1 9-inch unbaked pastry shell
1 cup flaked coconut

Blend eggs, flour, sugar, salt, and vanilla. Stir in coconut milk. Pour into unbaked pastry shell. Sprinkle top with flaked coconut. Bake at 350 degrees F for 60 minutes or until knife inserted in center comes out clean. Cool on rack, then chill.

Reduced Sugar Coconut Custard Pie

Make the Coconut Custard Pie as directed but reduce sugar to ¼ cup and add a dash or two of stevia or enough to suit your taste.

LEMON MERINGUE PIE ♥

1 can (14 ounces) coconut milk
1½ cups sugar
⅓ cup plus 1 tablespoon cornstarch
3 egg yolks, slightly beaten
3 tablespoons butter
½ teaspoon grated lemon peel
½ cup lemon juice
1 9-inch baked pastry shell
Meringue (page 175)

Preheat oven to 400 degrees F. Mix coconut milk, sugar, and cornstarch in saucepan. Cook over medium heat, stirring constantly, until mixture thickens and begins to boil. Cook and stir 1 minute. Remove from heat. Gradually stir at least half of the hot mixture into egg yolks and then stir egg yolks into the rest of the hot mixture in saucepan. Return to heat and cook for 1 minute, stirring constantly. Remove from heat; stir in butter, lemon peel, and lemon juice. Pour into baked pie shell. Spoon meringue on top of hot pie filling; spread over filling, carefully sealing meringue to edge of crust to prevent shrinking. Bake 10 minutes, until light brown. Cool on wire rack and then chill.

ORANGE MERINGUE PIE

1 can (14 ounces) coconut milk
1½ cups sugar
⅓ cup plus 1 tablespoon cornstarch
3 egg yolks, slightly beaten
3 tablespoons butter
1 teaspoon grated orange peel
¼ cup orange juice
¼ cup lemon juice
1 9-inch baked pastry shell
Meringue (page 175)

Preheat oven to 400 degrees F. Mix coconut milk, sugar, and cornstarch in saucepan. Cook over medium heat, stirring constantly, until mixture thickens and begins to boil. Cook and stir 1 minute. Remove from heat. Gradually stir at least half of the hot mixture into egg yolks and then stir egg yolks into the rest of the hot mixture in saucepan. Return to heat and cook for 1 minute, stirring constantly. Remove from heat; stir in butter, orange peel, orange juice, and lemon juice. Pour into baked pie shell. Spoon meringue on top of hot pie filling; spread over filling, carefully sealing meringue to edge of crust to prevent shrinking. Bake 10 minutes, until light brown. Cool and place in refrigerator. Serve chilled.

COCONUT LIME PIE

4 egg yolks
½ cup sugar
2 teaspoons salt
⅓ cup lime juice (2 to 3 limes)
1 cup Coconut Whipped Cream (page 175)
1 tablespoon grated lime peel
1 9-inch baked pastry shell

Beat egg yolkes together and put into a saucepan. Add sugar, salt, and lime juice. Cook over medium heat, stirring constantly until mixture thickens, about 5 minutes. Remove from heat and chill. Fold in Coconut Whipped Cream and grated lime peel. Spoon into baked pastry shell; refrigerate at least 4 hours. Top with Coconut Whipped Cream (page 175).

PUMPKIN PIE

1 can (15 to 16 ounces) pumpkin
¾ cup sugar
¾ teaspoon salt
1 teaspoon ground cinnamon
½ teaspoon ground ginger
¼ teaspoon ground nutmeg
¼ teaspoon ground cloves
3 slightly beaten eggs
1 cup coconut milk
1 9-inch unbaked pastry shell

Preheat oven to 400 degrees F. Mix together all ingredients and pour into pastry shell. The Coconut Pastry Shell (page 174) works well for this pie. Bake for 50 minutes or until knife inserted in center comes out clean. Cool. Just before serving top with Coconut Whipped Cream.

Sweet Potato Pie
Prepare Pumpkin Pie as directed but substitute 1½ cups of cooked mashed sweet potatoes for the pumpkin.

Reduced Sugar Pumpkin Pie
Make Pumpkin Pie as directed but reduce sugar to ½ cup, add ⅛ teaspoon stevia, and add 1 tablespoon flour.

COCONUT PECAN PIE ♥

4 beaten eggs
1 cup sugar
½ cup melted butter

4 teaspoons lemon juice
1 teaspoon vanilla
1 cup grated coconut
1 9-inch unbaked pastry shell
½ to ⅔ cup pecan halves

Beat eggs, sugar, melted butter, lemon juice, and vanilla together until well blended; stir in coconut. Pour into unbaked pie shell. Carefully layer pecan halves on top of pie filling. Bake at 350 degrees F for 40 minutes. Remove from oven and cool on wire rack. Filling will be slightly runny but will thicken as it cools.

Reduced Sugar Coconut Pecan Pie
Follow directions above but reduce sugar to ½ cup, add ⅛ teaspoon stevia, and reduce lemon juice to 3 teaspoons.

COCONUT ALMOND PIE

¼ cup butter, softened to room temperature
1 cup sugar
2 eggs
2 tablespoons flour
½ cup coconut milk
¼ teaspoon almond extract
1½ cups grated coconut
9-inch unbaked pastry shell
1 cup sliced or slivered almonds

Preheat oven to 350 degrees F. Cream butter and sugar until light, beat in eggs 1 at a time. Sprinkle in flour and blend until smooth. Mix in remaining ingredients and spoon into unbaked pastry shell. Sprinkle sliced almonds on top. Bake 45 minutes until browned and springy to the touch. Cool on a wire rack and serve at room temperature.

Reduced Sugar Coconut Almond Pie
Follow directions above but reduce sugar to ½ cup and add ⅛ teaspoon stevia.

COCONUT PEACH CRISP

Filling
5 to 6 peeled and sliced peaches
2 tablespoons flour
½ teaspoon cinnamon
¼ cup sucanat or brown sugar
Topping
¾ cup oats
¾ cup sucanat or brown sugar
½ cup flour
¾ cup flaked coconut
½ cup butter or coconut oil, softened
Dash of salt

In a bowl, mix peaches, flour, cinnamon, and sugar together. Arrange peach mixture in an 8x8x2-inch baking dish and set aside. Mix all the topping ingredients together and layer on top of the peaches. Bake at 400 degrees for 30 minutes. Serve topped with Coconut Whipped Cream (page 175).

Coconut Apple Crisp
Make Coconut Peach Crisp as directed but substitute tart apples for the peaches.

Reduced Sugar Coconut Peach Crisp
Make Coconut Peach Crisp as directed but delete the sugar from the peach mixture. Reduce sugar in topping to ¼ cup and add ⅛ teaspoon stevia.

FRUIT AND COCONUT COBBLER

1 cup flour
2 tablespoons sugar
½ cup grated coconut
1½ teaspoons baking powder
¼ teaspoon salt
¼ cup coconut oil, melted

¼ cup coconut milk
2 eggs, slightly beaten
Fruit filling (below)

All ingredients should be at room temperature so coconut oil mixes evenly. Mix together flour, sugar, coconut, baking powder, and salt. Add coconut oil, coconut milk, and eggs and stir just to moisten. Spoon dough on top of fruit filling. Bake at 400 degrees F for 25 to 30 minutes, until golden. Cool and serve with Coconut Whipped Cream (page 175).

Peach Filling

4 cups fresh sliced peaches
½ cup sugar
1 tablespoon cornstarch
¼ teaspoon ground cinnamon
1 teaspoon lemon juice
In a bowl mix sugar, cornstarch, cinnamon, and lemon juice together with ½ cup peach juice or water. Add in peaches and pour into baking dish, top with dough and cook as directed.

Cherry Filling

Follow the directions for Peach Filling, but substitute 4 cups pitted red tart cherries for the peaches and substitute ¼ teaspoon almond extract for the lemon juice.

Apple Filling

Follow the directions for Peach Filling, but substitute 4 cups sliced tart apples for the peaches, and add ¼ teaspoon nutmeg.

Reduced Sugar Cobbler

Make cobbler dough as directed but reduce sugar to ¼ cup and add ⅛ teaspoon of powdered stevia. Reduce sugar in Peach and Apple Fillings to ¼ cup or less. For the Cherry Filling, reduce sugar to ½ cup and use ¼ teaspoon of stevia in the batter.

CREAM PUFFS AND ECLAIRS

CREAM PUFFS

½ cup water
¼ cup butter
Dash of salt
½ cup flour
2 eggs
Cream Filling (below)

Preheat oven to 400 degrees F. In a saucepan heat water, butter, and salt to a boil. Add flour all at once, and stir vigorously over low heat until mixture forms a ball, about 1 minute. Remove from heat. Add the eggs all at once and continue beating until smooth. Mixture will look odd at first, almost like it's curdled, but as you beat, it will become smooth. Drop dough by scant ¼ cupfuls about 3 inches apart onto ungreased cookie sheet. Bake 35 to 40 minutes, until puffed and golden brown. Remove puffs from pan while still hot. Let cool. Cut off tops. Puffs will be hollow. Fill puffs with Cream Filling. Replace tops, sprinkle with powdered sugar. Keep refrigerated and serve chilled.

CREAM FILLINGS

Vanilla Cream Filling
1 can (14 ounces) coconut milk
⅓ cup sugar
¼ cup cornstarch
⅛ teaspoon salt
2 egg yolks, slightly beaten
2 tablespoons butter, softened
2 teaspoons vanilla

Mix coconut milk, sugar, cornstarch, and salt in large saucepan. Cook over medium heat, stirring constantly until mixture thickens. Boil and stir 1 minute. Stir at least half of the hot mixture slowly into egg yolks; stir back into hot mixture. Boil and stir 1 minute. Remove from heat; stir in butter and vanilla, cool.

Reduced Sugar Cream Filling

Make the Vanilla Cream Filling as directed but reduce sugar to 2 tablespoons and add a dash or two of stevia.

Banana Cream Filling

Make the Vanilla Cream Filling as directed but reduce sugar to 1 tablespoon and add ½ cup ripe mashed banana with the butter and vanilla. For reduced sugar version omit the sugar.

Almond Cream Filling

Make the Vanilla Cream Filling as directed but add 1 teaspoon almond extract along with the vanilla.

Chocolate Cream Filling

Make the Vanilla Cream Filling as directed but stir in 6 tablespoons of semisweet chocolate chips into mixture along with the butter and vanilla.

Caramel Cream Filling

Make the Vanilla Cream Filling as directed but substitute sucanat for the sugar.

Lemon Cream Filling

Make the Vanilla Cream Filling as directed but stir in ½ cup lemon juice into mixture along with the butter and vanilla.

CHOCOLATE ECLAIRS

Make cream puff dough as directed above. Drop dough by scant ¼ cupfuls onto ungreased cookie sheet. Shape each into logs 4½ inches long and 1½ inches wide with spatula. Bake and cool. Fill puffs with cream filling. Cover with Chocolate Frosting (below). Refrigerate and serve chilled.

Chocolate Frosting

Heat ½ square (½ ounce) unsweetened chocolate and ½ teaspoon butter over low heat until melted. Remove from heat; stir in ½ cup powdered sugar and about 1 tablespoon hot water. Beat until smooth.

CHAPTER 13

Puddings

COCONUT VANILLA PUDDING

2 tablespoons cornstarch
½ cup granulated white sugar
Dash of salt
1 can (14 ounces) coconut milk or cream
1 tablespoon butter
1 egg, lightly beaten
2 teaspoons vanilla
Flaked coconut, toasted

Mix cornstarch, sugar, and salt in a heavy saucepan. Gradually mix in milk and butter and heat, stirring constantly over moderate heat, until mixture boils. Boil and stir 1 minute. Remove from heat. Pour about 1 cup of hot mixture, very slowly, into the egg, stirring constantly. Return egg mixture to pan, and cook and stir 2 to 3 minutes until no raw taste of egg remains. Do not boil. Remove from heat. Stir in vanilla and let cool slightly. Pour into custard cups. Serve hot or chilled topped with toasted flaked coconut. Makes 3 servings.

Caramel Pudding
Prepare pudding as directed but substitute ¾ cup firmly packed dark brown sugar or sucanat for the granulated sugar.

Maple Pudding
Prepare pudding as directed but omit sugar and replace with powdered maple syrup.

Almond Pudding
Prepare pudding as directed but reduce vanilla to 1 teaspoon and add ½ teaspoon almond extract. Top with toasted sliced almonds.

Reduced Sugar Coconut Vanilla Pudding
Make Coconut Vanilla Pudding as directed but reduce sugar to ¼ cup and add a dash or two of powdered stevia.

CHOCOLATE PUDDING ♥

3 tablespoons cocoa
⅓ cup sugar

Dash of salt
3 tablespoons water
1 can (14 ounces) coconut milk or cream
2 tablespoons cornstarch
1 teaspoon vanilla

Mix cocoa, sugar, and salt in saucepan; stir in water. Cook and stir over medium heat until mixture boils; boil and stir 2 minutes. Mix coconut milk and cornstarch together using an electric mixer or wire whisk until blended. Pour into hot mixture stirring constantly. Continue to cook until mixture thickens, about 5 or 6 minutes. Remove from heat and blend in vanilla. Cool and pour into custard cups. Serve hot or cold. Top with toasted coconut flakes or toasted sliced almonds just before serving. Makes 3 servings.

HALF AND HALF PUDDING ♥

Make the Coconut Vanilla Pudding (page 191), fill custard cups half way, and chill. Make the Chocolate Pudding above and let cool. Pour the Chocolate Pudding into the center of the Coconut Vanilla Pudding (do not stir) and chill until set. Before serving, top with toasted flaked coconut or sliced almonds. Makes 6 servings.

BANANA PUDDING ♥

2 medium bananas, thinly sliced
1 can (14 ounces) coconut milk
¼ teaspoon ground cinnamon
1 teaspoon honey
Dash of salt
Shredded coconut, toasted

Combine bananas, coconut milk, cinnamon, honey, and salt in saucepan and heat to boiling. Reduce heat and simmer for about 8 minutes. Let cool. Can be eaten warm or cold. As it cools, pudding thickens. Serve with toasted coconut sprinkled on top.

COCONUT PUDDING SQUARES

This is a rich, sweet gelatinous dessert that is popular in Hawaii.

1 can (14 ounces) coconut milk
7 tablespoons sugar
7 tablespoons cornstarch
Dash of salt

Mix coconut milk, sugar, cornstarch, and salt in saucepan. Heat to boiling; reduce heat and simmer, stirring constantly until mixture thickens. Keep stirring on low heat until mixture become very thick and sticky. Pour into 8-inch pan and chill until firm. Cut into 2-inch squares and serve.

BROWN RICE PUDDING

½ cup uncooked brown rice
½ cup water
1 can (14 ounces) coconut milk
1 tablespoon honey
2 to 3 dashes of salt

Soak brown rice in ½ cup water for at least 4 hours or overnight. Add coconut milk, honey, and salt; bring to a boil, reduce heat, cover, and simmer for 40 minutes until rice is soft and most, but not all, of the liquid is absorbed. Serve hot. Makes a great lightly sweetened dessert or breakfast.

This recipe can be made with white rice if you prefer. If you use white rice, reduce cooking time to about 20 minutes.

Vanilla Rice Pudding
Follow the directions above but add 2 teaspoons vanilla after rice has been cooked.

Almond Rice Pudding
Add 1 teaspoon almond extract and ½ cup toasted slivered almonds after rice has been cooked.

Rice Pudding with Fresh Fruit
This recipe goes well mixed with fresh sliced fruit. Add the fruit to the rice after it is cooked. Fruits that go well include peaches, mangos, bananas, strawberries, blueberries, boysenberries, blackberries, raspberries, and pineapple.

Cinnamon Apple Rice Pudding
Add 1 teaspoon cinnamon and 1 chopped tart apple to the rice before cooking.

Cinnamon Raisin Rice Pudding
Add 1 teaspoon cinnamon and ½ cup raisins to rice before cooking.

BAKED CUSTARD

3 eggs
1 can (14 ounces) coconut milk
⅓ cup sugar
Dash of salt
1 teaspoon vanilla
Ground nutmeg

Preheat oven to 350 degrees F. Beat eggs lightly together with coconut milk, sugar, salt, and vanilla. Pour into six 6-ounce custard cups; sprinkle top with nutmeg. Place cups in baking dish about 13x9x2 inches in size. Pour very hot water into pan up to ½ inch from the tops of the custard cups. Bake for 45 minutes or until knife inserted in custard comes out clean. Remove cups from water and serve warm or chilled.

Maple Custard
Prepare custard as directed but substitute powdered maple syrup for the sugar.

Reduced Sugar Custard
Prepare custard as directed but reduce sugar to 3 tablespoons and add a dash or two of stevia.

TAPIOCA

½ cup quick cooking tapioca
3 cups coconut milk
½ cup sugar
¼ teaspoon salt

2 eggs, beaten
1 teaspoon vanilla

Heat tapioca, coconut milk, sugar, and salt in a saucepan. Stir until boiling, reduce heat to low and simmer 8 to 10 minutes, uncovered. Slowly stir half of the hot tapioca into the beaten eggs, then combine it with the other half of the hot mixture. Simmer, stirring constantly, until thickened. Remove from heat, add vanilla, and cool. Serve warm or chilled.

Chocolate Tapioca
Make tapioca as directed but add 2 ounces of unsweetened chocolate.

Reduced Sugar Tapioca
Make Tapioca according to directions but reduce sugar to ¼ cup and add a dash or two of powdered stevia.

FRUITY TAPIOCA PUDDING

½ cup sugar
¼ cup quick cooking tapioca
1¾ cups orange juice
¾ cup coconut milk
Dash of salt
1 orange, sectioned and cut into small bite-size pieces
¼ cup raisins or cut up dates
¼ cup flaked coconut

Mix sugar, tapioca, orange juice, coconut milk, and salt in large saucepan. Let stand 5 minutes. Heat to a boil, reduce heat, and simmer 8 minutes, stirring constantly. Remove from heat and add raisins. Cool slightly. Stir in orange sections. Refrigerate at least 1 hour. Sprinkle top with coconut and serve.

Reduced Sugar Fruity Tapioca Pudding
Make Fruity Tapioca Pudding as directed but omit the sugar and add ⅛ teaspoon powdered stevia.

CHAPTER 14

Ice Cream

HOMEMADE ICE CREAM

If you like coconut and you like ice cream, this chapter will be one of your favorites. The best way to make homemade ice cream is with an ice cream maker. Not everyone has an ice cream maker, therefore, I am including directions on how to make ice cream using a blender. The blender method makes a relatively smooth, delicious tasting ice cream. Ice cream makers, however, produce a much smoother, lighter product that is superior in taste and texture. If you plan on making a lot of ice cream—and you may once you try some of these recipes—I recommend buying an ice cream maker. They don't really cost that much and are well worth the price.

BASIC ICE CREAM RECIPES

You can choose from three basic vanilla ice cream recipes: Quick, Premium, and Reduced Sugar. All of the ice cream flavors described in this chapter can be made using any of these three basic recipes. The Quick recipe, as the name implies, is the simplest and easiest to make. The Premium recipe is made using eggs. It takes a little longer and requires a bit more care, but produces a smoother textured product that more closely resembles commercial ice cream. The Reduced Sugar recipe is for those people who want to enjoy the creamy richness and flavor of ice cream without all the sugar.

Because the three basic recipes are made using coconut milk or cream rather than dairy milk, they are each referred to as *Coconut* Vanilla Ice Cream rather than just vanilla ice cream. The coconut milk gives them a slightly different but great tasting flavor. Coconut Vanilla Ice Cream is used as the basis for all the flavors described in this chapter. Use whichever one of the three you want in making the various flavors that follow.

Homemade ice cream generally freezes a little harder than commercial ice cream. When first taken out of the freezer, it can be a bit difficult to scoop out. If you let it sit at room temperature for about 10 or 15 minutes, it will be much easier to work with.

QUICK COCONUT VANILLA ICE CREAM

1 can (14 ounces) coconut milk or cream
2 tablespoons sugar

Dash of salt
1 tablespoon vanilla

Put coconut milk, sugar, and salt in a saucepan. Heat at moderate to low temperature until ingredients are dissolved. Do not boil. Take off heat and stir in vanilla. If you have an ice cream maker, put the mixture into the refrigerator until chilled. Follow the directions given with your unit.

If you do not have an ice cream maker, pour the mixture into a freezer safe container and freeze. A convenient container is an ice cub tray. Freeze the mixture until it is mostly, but not completely, solid (about 2 hours). If the mixture becomes completely frozen, take it out of the freezer and let it sit at room temperature until it begins to melt. You want the mixture to be cold (about 32 degrees F) but not frozen solid. Put the mixture into a blender and turn it on. If the mixture is too hard, it will not blend well. Wait for it to warm up a little and try again. While blending, the mixture should take on the appearance and texture of a thick milkshake. Eat immediately or pour the ice cream into an airtight container and freeze. Blending the mixture and freezing it a second time like this crushes the ice crystals that form during the first freezing and gives the ice cream a smoother, creamier texture.

PREMIUM COCONUT VANILLA ICE CREAM

1 can (14 ounces) coconut milk or cream
¼ cup coconut oil (optional)*
2½ tablespoons sugar
Dash of salt
1 egg, beaten
1 tablespoon vanilla

Combine coconut milk, coconut oil, sugar, and salt in saucepan. Cook over medium heat, stirring occasionally until mixture almost boils. Reduce heat to low. In a bowl beat egg. Gradually stir about ½ cup of hot coconut milk into the beaten egg. Slowly stir this egg mixture into remaining hot coconut milk. Cook over low heat, stirring constantly until slightly thickened, about 2 to 3 minutes. Stir in vanilla. Remove from heat and let cool. Use the blender or ice cream maker method to finish.

*Coconut oil gives the ice cream a richer, creamier taste and texture, especially if you use coconut milk. It can be omitted if you use coconut cream.

198

REDUCED SUGAR COCONUT VANILLA ICE CREAM
Follow the directions for making either of the two Coconut Vanilla Ice Cream recipes but reduce sugar to 4 teaspoons or less and add a dash or two of stevia.

ICE CREAM FLAVORS
Use any of the three basic Coconut Vanilla Ice Cream recipes for the flavors described below. Unless otherwise noted, use one full recipe of Coconut Vanilla Ice Cream as the basis for all other flavors. The basic recipes make between 2 and 3 cups of ice cream depending on the method and version you use. Ice cream makers stir air into the mixture giving the ice cream greater volume. The Premium Coconut Vanilla Ice Cream made using an ice cream maker produces the best results for all flavors.

DOUBLE COCONUT ICE CREAM

1 full recipe Coconut Vanilla Ice Cream
1 teaspoon imitation coconut extract (optional)
¼ cup toasted flaked coconut

Make Coconut Vanilla Ice Cream according to directions adding imitation coconut extract along with the vanilla. Just before serving garnish with toasted flaked coconut.

COCONUT PINEAPPLE

1 full recipe Coconut Vanilla Ice Cream
1 ¼ cup crushed pineapple with juice
⅓ cup toasted flaked coconut

Make Coconut Vanilla Ice Cream according to directions. Place the pineapple in the refrigerator to chill (at least 1 hour). After removing the ice cream from the ice cream maker or blender, add the chilled crushed pineapple and mix thoroughly. Put immediately into the freezer to harden.

Place ⅓ cup of flaked coconut on a cookie sheet or glass baking dish. Spread the flakes out to make an even layer. Place in the oven at 350 degrees F for about 10 minutes or until golden brown. Just before serving the ice cream, sprinkle the top with the toasted coconut. Use freshly toasted coconut for best results.

ORANGE CREAM DELIGHT ♥

1 full recipe Coconut Vanilla Ice Cream
1 ¼ cup orange juice

Make Coconut Vanilla Ice Cream mixture according to directions. Before adding the mixture to the ice cream maker or blender combine with the orange juice. This recipe makes a delicious, creamy orange flavored ice cream.

CHOCOLATE ORANGE DELIGHT ♥

Follow the directions for the Orange Cream Delight above and freeze. Before serving, drizzle chocolate syrup on top. Enjoy!

FRUIT SHERBET

1 full recipe Coconut Vanilla Ice Cream
1 ¾ to 2 cups fruit juice

This recipe makes a delicious, sherbet-like fruit flavored ice cream. When the ice cream mixture is taken off the stove, add 1 ¾ to 2 cups of fruit juice. Different brands of juice vary in flavor and sweetness so taste the mixture and add more juice or sugar to suit your taste. Finish by using the blender or ice cream maker method. Makes about 4 cups.

Almost any kind of fruit juice will work in this recipe. Stores, and particularly health food stores, carry a wide selection of bottled and frozen fruit juices. Some of the juices I've seen include orange, lime, lemon, peach, papaya, guava, mango, apricot, cherry, cranberry, raspberry, orange mango, blueberry, grape, cranberry grape, pineapple, and even coconut nectar. Some juices are very sweet and you may want to reduce the sugar in the original recipe to 1 tablespoon or less and adjust sweetness after you add the juice.

FRUIT FLAVORED ICE CREAM

1 full recipe Coconut Vanilla Ice Cream
½ cup frozen fruit juice concentrate, no added water

This makes a delicious, creamy fruit flavored ice cream. This recipe has less water than the Fruit Sherbet described above, allowing the finished product to have a higher percentage of coconut cream. Almost any flavor of frozen fruit juice concentrate works with this recipe.

Make Coconut Vanilla Ice Cream according to directions. When all the ingredients have been combined on the stove, remove the mixture from the heat and let cool. While cooling, add ½ cup of frozen fruit juice concentrate, without added water. Let it melt and mix thoroughly. Finish by using the blender or ice cream maker method. Makes about 2½ cups.

COCONUT SHERBET

This very simple and easy sherbet is made with young coconut water rather than coconut milk or cream. For best results use coconut water from immature or green coconuts rather than the juice from a mature coconut. If you don't have access to fresh young coconuts, you can use commercially produced coconut water.

All you need for this sherbet is coconut water and an ice cream maker. Let the ice cream maker churn and freeze the water into a sherbet just as you would any other sherbet. There is no need to add sugar or anything else. The end product is a delicious tasting coconut sherbet.

STRAWBERRY ICE CREAM ♥

1 full recipe Coconut Vanilla Ice Cream
1½ to 2 cups strawberries

Make Coconut Vanilla Ice Cream as described but increase sugar to 3 tablespoons. Before freezing or putting mixture into an ice cream maker, add fresh or frozen strawberries and blend in a blender. Taste for sweetness and add more sugar if needed. Finish by using the ice cream maker or blender method.

Fresh Fruit Ice Cream

A variety of fruit ice creams can be made using the recipe above with different fresh fruits. Some good ones include raspberries, blackberries, blueberries, cherries, and peaches. Ripeness and sweetness varies so you may need to adjust sugar content.

CHUNKY CHOCOLATE ALMOND ♥

1 cup toasted almonds
5 tablespoons chocolate syrup
1 full recipe Coconut Vanilla Ice Cream
1 teaspoon almond extract

Preheat oven to 325 degrees F. Toast whole or chopped almonds for 10-15 minutes or until slightly browned. Stir the toasted almonds into the chocolate and set aside to cool. Make the Coconut Vanilla Ice Cream recipe according to directions, but add 1 teaspoon of almond extract at the same time as the vanilla. The chocolate almond mixture should be at room temperature or cooler before adding to the ice cream. Just before placing the ice cream into the freezer, add the chocolate almond mixture a spoonful at a time. Stir a couple of times to evenly distribute the chocolate and almond chucks and freeze.

PEPPERMINT

1 full recipe Coconut Vanilla Ice Cream
1 teaspoon peppermint extract
¼ cup crushed peppermint candy (optional)

Make the Coconut Vanilla Ice Cream recipe according to directions, but add 1 teaspoon of peppermint extract at the same time as the vanilla. After the ice cream is churned and just before freezing, mix in crushed peppermint candy.

MAPLE NUT

1 full recipe Coconut Vanilla Ice Cream
3 tablespoons maple syrup
¼ cup walnuts or black walnuts, chopped

Make the Coconut Vanilla Ice Cream according to directions, substituting 3 tablespoons of maple syrup for the sugar. Just before freezing, mix in chopped nuts.

CHOCOLATE ICE CREAM (Basic Recipe)

¼ cup coconut oil
3 tablespoons cocoa
1¾ cups coconut milk or cream
Dash of salt
⅓ cup sugar
1 tablespoon vanilla

This is a basic recipe you can use for any variety of chocolate ice cream. Melt coconut oil in a sauce pan at low heat. Add cocoa powder and mix thoroughly. Keep the cocoa mixture on low heat, stirring frequently; be careful not to boil. In a second saucepan heat coconut milk, salt, and, sugar until the sugar is completely dissolved. With the cocoa mixture on low heat, slowly pour into it the coconut milk mixture while stirring. Continue to stir until the mixtures blend, forming a smooth, creamy chocolate. Add vanilla. Finish by using the ice cream maker or blender method.

Quick Chocolate Ice Cream
A quick and easy method of making chocolate ice cream is to add ⅓ cup of chocolate syrup to the Coconut Vanilla Ice Cream before putting it into the ice cream maker.

ROCKY ROAD ♥

1 full recipe Chocolate Ice Cream
¾ cup miniature marshmallows
½ cup chopped nuts

Make the Chocolate Ice Cream recipe according to directions. Before putting the ice cream into the freezer, stir in marshmallows and nuts.

CHOCOLATE MARSHMALLOW SWIRL ♥

¾ cup toasted almonds
1 full recipe Chocolate Ice Cream
1 cup marshmallow cream

Preheat oven to 325 degrees F. Toast whole or chopped almonds for 10-15 minutes or until slightly browned. Set aside to cool. Make the Chocolate Ice Cream recipe according to directions. Before freezing the ice cream, add marshmallow cream and toasted almonds and stir them in just enough to create a swirl effect.

TOFFEE CHOCOLATE CHIP

1 full recipe Coconut Vanilla Ice Cream
½ teaspoon almond extract
⅓ cup English toffee bits
½ cup milk chocolate chips

Make Coconut Vanilla Ice Cream according to directions and add almond extract with vanilla. Before putting into freezer, mix in toffee bits and chocolate chips.

FRIED ICE CREAM ♥

1 full recipe Coconut Vanilla Ice Cream
½ cup toasted sliced almonds
½ cup toasted coconut flakes
¼ cup honey

The secret to Fried Ice Cream is in the making of the crust. The crust in this recipe consists of toasted almonds and coconut. Sliced almonds work best, but you may use slivered or even chopped whole almonds as well. Unlike the name implies, this ice cream isn't actually fried. It is coated in a layer of toasted almonds and coconut. Traditionally vanilla ice cream is used, but strawberry or chocolate ice cream also taste great.

Make Coconut Vanilla Ice Cream according to directions and freeze (at least 3 hours). Before serving, preheat oven to 325 degrees F. Place sliced almonds and coconut flakes in a single layer on a cookie sheet or baking dish. Bake in the oven for about 10 minutes or until coconut is golden brown. Remove from oven and cool. Scoop ice cream out in serving-sized balls. Roll balls in toasted coating or simply sprinkle the coating on the ice cream. Use a generous amount of coating; sprinkle the remaining coating along the sides of the bowl. Drizzle a little honey on top and serve.

FUDGESICLE ICE CREAM
This ice cream tastes just like the fudgesicles you buy in the store.

¼ cup sugar
2 tablespoons cocoa
Dash of salt
3 tablespoons water
1 can (14 ounces) coconut milk or cream
½ teaspoon vanilla

Mix sugar, cocoa, and salt in saucepan; stir in water. Stir over medium heat until mixture boils and sugar dissolves. Stir in coconut milk or cream. Remove from heat; add vanilla. Let cool. Store in freezer.

FROZEN CHOCOLATE BANANAS

1 package (6 ounces) semisweet chocolate chips
2 tablespoons coconut oil
2 bananas, halved crosswise
4 wooden sticks
½ cup toasted flaked coconut

Line a baking sheet or plate with wax paper. Insert wooden sticks into banana halves, place on wax paper, and put in freezer overnight or until frozen. In a small, heavy saucepan, melt chocolate and coconut oil over very low heat, stirring constantly. When melted, remove from heat and let cool to room temperature. The mixture should still be soft. Remove bananas from freezer and dip them in the chocolate, spreading the chocolate to form a fairly even coat. Immediately roll in toasted coconut and place back on wax paper. Freeze for at least 30 minutes. If not eaten that day, store in an airtight container.

Favorite Coconut Recipes
Add your favorite coconut recipes from other sources here.

Favorite Coconut Recipes

Favorite Coconut Recipes

Favorite Coconut Recipes

Favorite Coconut Recipes

Favorite Coconut Recipes

Favorite Coconut Recipes

Index

Chicken and rice stew, 80
Chicken and sweet potato stew with
coconut dumplings, 120
Chicken and vegetables in cream
sauce, 109
Chicken gravy, 60
Chicken in curry sauce, 108
Chicken in red curry sauce, 114
Chicken linguine, 90
Chicken pot pie, 88
Chicken rice casserole, 97
Chicken stir-fry, 87
Chocolate almond, 26
Chocolate coconut bars, 165
Chocolate coconut cream filling, 156
Chocolate coconut oatmeal cookies,
163
Chocolate cream filling, 189
Chocolate cream pie, 178
Chocolate crispies, 169
Chocolate crisps, 169
Chocolate eclairs, 189
Chocolate frosting, 189
Chocolate fruit smoothie, 33
Chocolate granola bars, 170
Chocolate haystacks, 168
Chocolate ice cream, 203
Chocolate macaroons, 159
Chocolate marshmallow swirl, 204
Chocolate mint, 26
Chocolate orange delight, 200
Chocolate peanut butter smoothie,
34
Chocolate pudding, 191
Chocolate tapioca, 195
Chocolate whipped cream, 176
Chunky chicken gravy, 61
Chunky chocolate almond, 202
Cinnamon eggnog, 27
Cinnamon apple coconut cake, 157

Cinnamon nut muffins, 135
Cinnamon apple rice pudding, 194
Cinnamon raisin rice pudding, 194
Citrus cream filling, 156
Citrus refresher, 34
Coconut
  angel flake, 6
  butter, 14
  cream, 13
   homemade, 21
  desiccated, 6
  dried, 6-7, 11
  flaked, 6-7
  freeze-dried, 11
  grated, 6-7
  meat, 9-10, 15
  milk, 12, 13-14, 15, 35
   homemade, 21
  oil, 14-18, 35
  opening, 10-11
  shredded, 6-7
  water, 12-13, 15, 23, 31
Coconut almond macaroons, 159
Coconut almond pie, 185
Coconut apple crisp, 186
Coconut banana bread with lime
  glaze, 145
Coconut banana pancakes, 138
Coconut battered shrimp, 101
Coconut bran muffins, 133
Coconut butter cookies, 171
Coconut cake, 149
Coconut carrot cake, 152
Coconut chicken soup, 119
Coconut corn bread muffins, 135
Coconut corn chips, 131
Coconut cream cake, 155
Coconut cream cake filling, 156
Coconut cream pie, 178
Coconut custard pie, 182

Cooking With Coconut Flour

Do you love breads, cakes, pies, cookies, and other wheat products but can't eat them because you are allergic to wheat or sensitive to gluten? Perhaps you avoid wheat because you are concerned about your weight

and need to cut down on carbohydrates. If so, the solution for you is coconut flour. Coconut flour is a delicious, healthy alternative to wheat. It is high in fiber, low in digestible carbohydrate, and a good source of protein. It contains no gluten so it is ideal for those with celiac disease.

Coconut flour can be used to make a variety of delicious baked goods, snacks, desserts, and main dishes. It is the only flour used in most of the recipes in this book. These recipes are so delicious that you won't be able to tell that they aren't made with wheat. If you like foods such as German chocolate cake, apple pie, blueberry muffins, cheese crackers, and chicken

pot pie, but don't want the wheat, you will love the recipes in this book!

These recipes are designed with your health in mind. Every recipe is completely free of wheat, gluten, soy, trans fats, and artificial sweeteners. Coconut is naturally low in carbohydrate and recipes include both regular and reduced sugar versions. Coconut flour provides many health benefits. It can improve digestion, help regulate blood sugar, protect against diabetes, help prevent heart disease and cancer, and aid in weight loss. Coconut flour is a healthy and tasty alternative to wheat.

Coconut Water for Health and Healing

Coconut water is a refreshing beverage that comes from coconuts. It's a powerhouse of nutrition containing a complex blend of vitamins, minerals, amino acids, carbohydrates, antioxidants, enzymes, health enhancing growth hormones, and other phytonutrients.

Because its electrolyte (ionic mineral) content is similar to human plasma, it has gained international acclaim as a natural sports drink for oral rehydration. As such, it has proven superior to commercial sports drinks. Unlike other beverages, it is completely compatible with the human body, in so much that it can be infused directly into the bloodstream. In fact, doctors have used coconut water successfully as an intravenous fluid for over 60 years.

Coconut water's unique nutritional profile gives it the power to balance body chemistry, ward off disease, fight cancer, and retard aging. History and folklore credit coconut water with remarkable healing powers, which medical science is now confirming. Published medical research and clinical observation have shown that coconut water:

- Makes an excellent oral rehydration sports beverage
- Aids in exercise performance
- Reduces swelling in hands and feet
- Aids in kidney function and dissolves kidney stones
- Protects against cancer
- Helps balance blood sugar in diabetics
- Provides a source of ionic trace minerals
- Improves digestion
- Contains nutrients that feed friendly gut bacteria
- Helps relieve constipation
- Reduces risk of heart disease
- Improves blood circulation
- Lowers high blood pressure
- Improves blood cholesterol levels

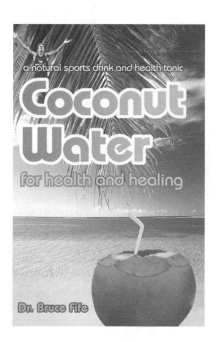

Coconut Cures

You've heard about the healing power coconut oil but did you know that the entire coconut is a virtual medicine chest? Coconut meat, milk, and water all have medicinal as well as nutritional value. The health benefits of the entire coconut—the meat, milk, water, as well as the oil are explained in *Coconut Cures: Preventing and Treating Common Health Problems with Coconut.*

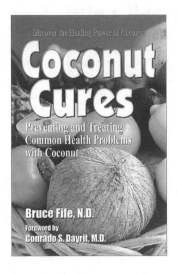

This book describes why coconut water can and is used as an IV solution for sick patients. Coconut water has a chemical composition similar to human plasma and can be injected directly into the blood steam. Recent research has shown that it can be just as effective as commercial IV solutions. Coconut water is a delicious beverage loaded with vitamins and minerals. For this reason, it is fast gaining a reputation as an effective natural sports drink, superior to commercial beverages and lower in sugar. Its healing properties are most evident in the urinary and reproductive system. In Asia it is taken orally to dissolve kidney stones and restore libido. It has a restorative effect on the kidneys and some patients have been able to reduce or eliminate dialysis treatments simply by drinking coconut water.

Coconut meat is a virtual powerhouse of health. It can help balance blood sugar and control diabetes, protect against cancer, ease the pain and discomfort of colitis and irritable bowel syndrome, aid in weight loss, expel intestinal parasites, improve digestive function, help eliminate hemorrhoids and varicose veins, the list goes on an on.

Some of this information is so incredible you wouldn't believe it unless proof was provided, and the author does just that. Every health claim made in this book is backed by medical science. References to published studies are provided along with dozens of case studies and success stores.

This book isn't just a discussion of the benefits of coconut, it provides step-by-step instructions on how to use coconut to treat many common health problems. It includes an extensive A to Z listing of health problems and how to treat each one using various forms of coconut.

EAT FAT, LOOK THIN

You can enjoy rich, full-fat foods and lose weight without the hassle of counting calories, weighing portions, or suffering from hunger.

This book exposes many common myths and misconceptions about fats. It reveals new, cutting-edge research on the world's only natural, low-calorie fat-a fat that not only has fewer calories than any other fat, but one which also stimulates metabolism and burns up calories. Yes, you can lose weight by eating fat, if you use the right kind. Combined with a sensible eating plan, you can shed excess weight, enjoy the foods you love, and gain better health.

This revolutionary, total-wellness program is designed to keep you both slim and healthy using wholesome, natural foods, and the most health-promoting fats. It has proven successful in helping those suffering from obesity, diabetes, hypoglycemia, heart and circulatory problems, yeast infections, chronic fatigue, and many other conditions.

You will learn:

- Why low-fat diets don't work
- How to make dieting enjoyable
- How to use the world's only natural, low-calorie fat to lose weight
- Which fats promote health and which ones don't (the answers may surprise you)
- How to jump-start your metabolism
- How to stop food cravings dead cold
- How you can use food to overcome common health problems
- How to reach your ideal weight and stay there
- Why eating rich, delicious foods can help you lose weight
- Which foods are the real trouble-makers and how to avoid them.

For more information about these and other books on coconut, nutrition, and health write to Piccadilly Books, Ltd., P.O. Box 25203, Colorado Springs, CO 80936, USA or orders@piccadillybooks.com and ask for a free copy of the Healthy Ways catalog.

THE COCONUT OIL MIRACLE _____

Dr. Fife was the first person to gather together all the medical research on coconut oil and present it in a readable and understandable format. This best-selling book describes the many health benefits of coconut oil and dispells the untruths surrounding this often misunderstood oil.

Coconut oil has been called the healthiest dietary oil on earth. If you're not using coconut oil for your daily cooking and body care needs you're missing out on one of nature's most amazing health products. In this book you will discover the miracles of coconut oil. Each health benefit is explained and fully documented by scientific research.

Use nature's elixir to:
• lose weight • prevent heart disease, cancer, and diabetes • strengthen the immune system • beautify skin and hair

BRUCE FIFE, C.N., N.D.
Foreword by Jon J. Kabara, Ph.D.
Previously published as *The Healing Miracles of Coconut Oil*

Benefits of Coconut Oil include:

- Reduces risk of atherosclerosis and heart disease
- Reduces risk of cancer and other degenerative conditions
- Helps prevent bacterial, viral, and fungal (including yeast) infections
- Supports immune system function
- Helps prevent osteoporosis
- Helps control diabetes
- Promotes weight loss
- Provides an immediate source of energy
- Supplies fewer calories than other fats

- Improves digestion and nutrient absorption
- Has a mild delicate flavor
- Is highly resistant to spoilage (long shelf life)
- Is heat resistant (the healthiest oil for cooking)
- Helps keep skin soft and smooth
- Helps prevent premature aging and wrinkling of the skin
- Helps protect against skin cancer and other blemishes

Visit us on the Web

Piccadilly Books, Ltd.
www.piccadillybooks.com